SHARING THE OCEAN

Stories of Science, Politics, and Ownership from America's Oldest Industry

Michael Crocker

Photography by Rebecca Hale

Tilbury House, Publishers
Gardiner, Maine

Northwest Atlantic Marine Alliance
Windham, Maine

Tilbury House, Publishers
8 Mechanic Street, Gardiner, Maine 04345
800–582–1899 • www.tilburyhouse.com

Northwest Atlantic Marine Alliance
PO Box 360, Windham, Maine 04062
207-284-5374 • www.namanet.org

First paperback edition: July 2008
10 9 8 7 6 5 4 3 2 1

Library of Congress Cataloging-in-Publication Data
Crocker, Michael, 1976-
Sharing the ocean : stories of science, politics, and ownership from America's oldest industry
/ Michael Crocker ; photography by Rebecca Hale. — 1st paperback ed.
    p. cm.
Includes bibliographical references and index.
ISBN 978-0-88448-306-9 (pbk. : alk. paper)
1. Groundfish fisheries—New England—Management. 2. Groundfish fisheries—
Economic aspects—United States. 3. Fishery policy—United States. I. Title.
SH221.5.N4C76 2008
338.3'72717770973—dc22
                            2008005393

Cover photographs by Rebecca Hale
Design by Geraldine Millham, Westport, Massachusetts
Copyediting by Dorcas Miller, Chelsea, Maine
Printed and bound by J. S. McCarthy, Printers, Augusta, Maine
Printed on elemental chlorine free with 25 percent post-consumer recycled content paper
made with FSC certified wood pulp, with non-toxic vegetable-based ink, and employing
100 percent wind power.

For Craig and Peter. We would all do well to follow your example of collaboration.

CONTENTS

FOREWORD

The story of the New England groundfish fishery is one of boom and bust, of big profits and stunning collapses, and the struggle to find a balance between environmental stewardship and the financial stability of an industry with deep ties to the region's economy, politics, and identity. It's a story of men and women with a deep connection to the ocean and an honest desire to protect it, who at the same time have participated in overfishing and pushed one of the world's most productive resources to the brink of collapse. Blame is easy to assign: to fishermen for greed, to regulators for indifference, to environmentalists for callousness in the face of human tragedy, and to all for willful misunderstanding in favor of short-term self-interest.

Sharing the Ocean takes none of these routes. Mike Crocker does not pull his punches, but this straightforward recounting of the New England groundfish story from 1977 to the present identifies no villains. Rather, it tells the fascinating and often tragic story of how well-intentioned but deeply flawed management strategies pushed by the U.S. government and mainstream environmentalists have, in Crocker's words, "paradoxically sustained the ecological crisis and led to an unjust distribution of access to the fishery." Crocker draws on diverse economic, political, anthropological, and other sources to critique the philosophy and implementation of these management practices.

During my long career as a public servant in Maine, I have watched the rise and fall of the groundfish industry, from the fishing boom of the 1980s, to the collapse of stocks in the late 1980s and early 1990s, to the current struggle to rebuild. Like many of the fishermen, scientists, and conservationists featured in this book, I have had to make tough decisions about how to balance environmental protection with the economic welfare of the fishing industry, and I have watched some lose their livelihoods. I have fought for legislation to preserve access to the fishery for the smaller vessel owners and operators, those who have felt every fluctuation in stock abundance and suffered under every new regulatory restriction. I have also worked with men and women who have given up on ever making significant profits themselves and instead are fighting for hope and opportunities for their children and grandchildren to make a living from the sea. Throughout these ups and downs, I have been deeply impressed by the courage, character, and resilience of Maine's fishing community.

That is why you should read this book. *Sharing the Ocean* is an honest and moving portrait of those men and women, with all their diverse histories, dreams, and motivations. I hope that readers will be inspired by the dedication, environmental ethic, and self-sacrifice of these individuals, and outraged at the management failures that have decimated fish populations and are forcing fishermen out of business. The loss of this vibrant fishing community would be a tragedy, and Mike Crocker's book is a passionate and articulate call to reverse course and protect this important part of Maine and New England's heritage.

Thomas H. Allen
Member of Congress

ACKNOWLEDGMENTS

This book was very much the product of a collaborative effort and special gratitude should be extended to a number of people who were particularly generous with their time and knowledge. First, thanks to all who agreed to participate in the Fleet Visioning Project, especially those who gave additional time to sit for the portraits, and to Becky Hale for capturing the remarkable images in the final chapter. The Andrus Family Fund provided financial and moral support throughout the project and during the completion of this work. The philanthropy's unique level of personal involvement in its programs is unique in my experience with private foundations and a model others would do well to replicate. Steven Kelban, Sabena Leake, and Ken Downes, in particular, always made themselves available for key consultation and, more importantly, became friends over the course of our collaboration. Thank you also to Dr. Jay Rothman and Meghan Clarke of the Aria Group. Their experience and knowledge of conflict resolution in a variety of settings at home and abroad was invaluable to the design and implementation of the project.

I would also like to recognize the valuable advice given to me by Chris Weiner while I conducted research for the book. At the time he was a senior government major at Bowdoin College as well as an accomplished tuna fisherman. He wrote a thesis on the Magnuson–Steven Act and his familiarity with reference materials was extremely useful. Jennifer Plummer, NAMA's administrative coordinator, also provided invaluable and timely assistance. Finally, I would like to thank the NAMA Board of Trustees. Many of the fishermen, scientists, and environmentalists have been involved with the organization since its inception. Their long-term commitment to protecting fish resources and the people who harvest them is an inspiration.

INTRODUCTION

"We need to say no to the neoliberal fatalism that we are witnessing at the end of this century, informed by the ethics of the market, an ethics in which a minority makes most profits against the lives of the majority. In other words, those who cannot compete, die. This is a perverse ethics that, in fact, lacks ethics. I insist on saying that I continue to be human…I would then remain the last educator in the world to say no: I do not accept…history as determinism. I embrace history as possibility [where] we can demystify the evil in this perverse fatalism that characterizes the neoliberal discourse in the end of this century." —Paulo Freire

This project began with a paradox I could not resolve. Growing up in New England, in the 1980s, I became very concerned about the environmental health of the places I primarily used for recreation: rivers, streams, ocean, and mountains. Later, as an undergraduate, I spent a semester in northwest Montana studying grizzly bear habitat. After witnessing firsthand the devastating effects ecological degradation can have on a fragile species like bears, the experience added new urgency to my concerns. Montana had such an impact on me I went back there to attend graduate school. But it wasn't until I returned home for a job in Maine, writing about research that pairs commercial fishermen and scientists, that I came to appreciate the outdoors as a place where some people must work for a living.

Commercial fishing is a dangerous and complicated job that challenges all mental faculties and the limits of physical endurance. It is also, for long stretches at a time, unbearably boring. After leaving port, captains must steam many hours to reach productive fishing grounds. As groundfish stocks—cod, haddock, flounder, and other bottom-dwelling species—became scarce in the late 1980s boats were forced to venture even farther from shore.[1]

Once fish are located by a dragger, the fishery's principal gear-type, the decks become alive with frantic energy as a net is spooled off a drum set above the stern with steel cables and heavy iron doors that keep its mouth open as it is dragged across the bottom. The pace of work diminishes substantially after the captain settles on a location to tow the trawl, his focus shifting to a monitor that displays an electronic image of sound waves bounced off the seafloor. The return signal illustrates the rugged landscape beneath the waves: jagged spires, steep cliffs, and flat bottom appear as large arrhythmic fibrillations on an electrocardiogram. In the spaces between, foggy patches of static—schools of fish—can be found. With uncanny accuracy, some fishermen can decipher how many and what species are indicated by the flicker of light.

During tows, which can last for three or more hours, fishermen typically occupy themselves by reading *Commercial Fisheries News*, gossiping on the VHF radio and, if someone is there to listen, by talking. During these conversations I was repeatedly struck by the deep understanding fishermen have of marine ecology. Many keep detailed notes about how subtle changes in temperature, weather, and the phase of the moon affect the abundance and distribution of fishes that would put most oceanographers to shame.

But the discussions became even more passionate when the subject shifted to the National Marine Fisheries Service (NMFS, or "nymphs" as it is usually pronounced), the agency responsible for regulating the industry. NMFS assumed management responsibility after the Fisheries Conservation and Management Act was implemented in 1977.[2] The law expelled thousands of foreign fishing vessels, some 400 feet in length, from U.S. waters to protect several groundfish stocks on the brink of collapse.[3] It also initiated an economic development program that provided valuable subsidies to the fleet. The cheap money quickly transformed what was once a humble enterprise into big business and to a large extent introduced the absentee-owner, an investor more interested in turning a profit onshore than deriving a livelihood from the sea. Between 1977 and 1986 the fleet's killing power more than doubled. In 1989, only a decade after the government took control of the fishery in order to save it, officials announced that the stocks had collapsed again.[4]

In light of this conspicuous history I was not surprised to hear fishermen calling for a radically new approach to management, but the solution many proposed was as perplexing as it was intriguing. They insisted that fishermen—not the government—were the only people with the ecological knowledge and conservation ethic needed to effectively take care of the ocean. They spoke of ideas I had previously known only in the abstract: local knowledge, stewardship, community governance, and environmental justice. It all sounded well and good, but again that paradox:

how could fisherman—people with reason to kill every last fish in the sea—become responsible stewards? I needed more convincing.

In addition to claiming ocean resources between 3 and 200 miles of the U.S. coast (states maintained jurisdiction inside 3 miles), the fisheries legislation established eight regional councils to develop management plans for stocks in the Atlantic, Pacific, and Gulf of Mexico. The law technically made the councils subordinate to the admonitions of NMFS scientists, but ambiguity in the charter led to a relationship between the government agency and the quasi-private councils characterized by antagonism and miscommunication.[5] The New England Fishery Management Council is responsible for the day-to-day management of groundfish and several other species found in federal waters from New Jersey to Maine.

My first experience with the council came at the height of a management controversy, a public hearing on Amendment 13, in the spring of 2003. The proposed changes to the region's groundfish management plan were prompted by a decade-old lawsuit filed by the Conservation Law Foundation and other environmental groups against NMFS and the Department of Commerce (the agency's home inside the federal bureaucracy) for failing to prevent overfishing. The lawsuit eventually led to the adoption of a management strategy known as days-at-sea, which tries to reduce overfishing by restricting the time vessels are allowed to spend on the water. Initially, fishermen received an allocation of fishing days based on the amount of time they could prove they had spent on the water: in almost every case, more landings led to a greater allocation of days-at-sea.[6]

The streets outside the seaside hotel in Gloucester, Massachusetts, that hosted the meeting were jammed with boisterous demonstrators. Some held signs that proclaimed: "Fishermen: the Real Endangered Species!" Inside, the deliberations were repeatedly interrupted by shouts from the audience. An economist from the Conservation Law Foundation was berated with insults as she made her presentation. A tall and wiry fisherman with a white beard stepped up to the microphone and sang a lament about the loss of New England's proud fishing heritage. I nervously approached the podium, read from my notes, and returned to my seat. I didn't know much about fishing, but it was clear to me that the management process was terribly broken. I was ready to hear about the alternative the fishermen proposed.

Community-based management, as it is generally called, differs substantially from the strategy typically advanced by policymakers and mainstream environmentalists. Its adherents argue that the fishery crisis is the consequence of ill-conceived management policies, not unbridled fishermen's greed, as many have assumed.

(Community-based management is not, however, related to the conservative anti-federalist movement. That variety of decentralization confuses local control with private ownership. It is the ideology of people in power.) But neither does the community-based management movement constitute an attack on the political right by the radical left, for the same ideology characterizes the right and the left. It is therefore a kind of critique on the center of our culture and history.

The alternative, which is sometimes called area management, is grounded in the latest insights from ecology, economics, history, and anthropology. This information has shown that the fishery—its fish and its fishermen—are more dynamic and more diverse than is recognized by the current management protocol. Put simply, area management strives for ecological resilience and social equity by drawing management boundaries based on real biological divisions rather than arbitrary political lines. Fishermen are required to commit to one of these bioregions for several years to promote long-term stewardship. The idea is to end "pulse fishing," where highly mobile vessels overexploit large aggregations of fish across hundreds of miles of ocean, by making captains responsible for the long-term consequences of their fishing practices.[7]

The ecological justification for area management is the commonsense observation, supported by empirical evidence, that the biology of the Gulf of Maine—the large oceanic bight between Nantucket Shoals and the waters of Nova Scotia—is influenced by five major terrestrial features: Georges Bank, Cape Cod, Cape Ann, Penobscot Bay, and the continental shelf (what fishermen call "the edge of the bottom" or the 50-fathom curve). Numerous studies show that each area exhibits distinct oceanographic characteristics—such as bottom substrate, water density, dissolved oxygen levels, current patterns, and water clarity—that profoundly shape the survival and distribution of fish larvae, food availability, and the genetic traits of fish.[8]

This conception of the marine system, however, differs substantially from that employed by NMFS. Indeed, for some forty years, the agency has measured the abundance of groundfish using large research vessels and commercial-style fishing gear. To ensure statistical integrity, the approach begins by assuming that fish are spread homogeneously across the ocean. "Stations" randomly selected by a computer are then sampled according to several different depth categories, or strata.

The information is then extrapolated to calculate the population of groundfish stocks in four management areas: Southern New England, Eastern and Western Georges Bank, and the Gulf of Maine. From this number, scientists subtract the amount of fish they know to have already been extracted, as indicated by compulsory landings reports from fishermen and seafood dealers. A computer model is then used to integrate other data, such as estimates of losses due to natural predation and weather events, and a total mortality rate (known as "F") is calculated. The figure provides the scientific justification for the total allowable catch (or TAC) the agency recommends to the council for management each season.[9]

But, increasingly, fishermen and scientists have argued that the government's stock assessment protocol is at odds with ecological reality and the fishing practices of the fleet. Here's the problem as they see it: if there are more genetically distinct populations of cod, for example, than the fishing rules recognize—off Long Island, New York, the inshore Gulf of Maine, and the coastal waters east of Penobscot Bay, as the evidence suggests—then the recommended harvests set for the larger "meta-populations" in the management areas recognized by NMFS are likely far too great for these local stocks to support. After all, fishermen recognize the existence of the aggregations, drawing on their knowledge of ecology to locate fish in the times and places when they are most abundant. Scientists now believe a similar misapprehension led to the collapse of Newfoundland's cod fishery, which some fifteen years after a fishing moratorium was enacted, has still not recovered to commercially sustainable levels.[10]

The problem, however, is even more complex than I have been able to describe so far. The New England council has a long history of ignoring scientific advice in the face of overwhelming pressure from its constituency, which today is dominated by three main interest groups: fishermen, scientists, and environmentalists. It is the responsibility of NMFS scientists to determine how many fish can be harvested and, by extension, the prosperity of the industry. But the accuracy of these assessments has frequently been called into question, and several public blunders have undermined many fishermen's faith in the system.[11]

Environmentalists didn't really enter the fray until the early 1990s, when a lawsuit forced the government to dramatically cut back fishing effort. In many cases, the rules have slowed the pace of ecological degradation, but at the cost of hundreds of lost livelihoods, particularly in rural communities. The social impact of environmentalism has built up distrust between fishermen and environmentalists, overshadowing many of the conservation goals shared by the two groups.

Finally, there are the fishermen. Popular stereotypes depict the industry as a homogeneous group united in opposition to regulations. In fact, fishermen are very much divided by operational scales, gear-types, access to wealth and power, fishing

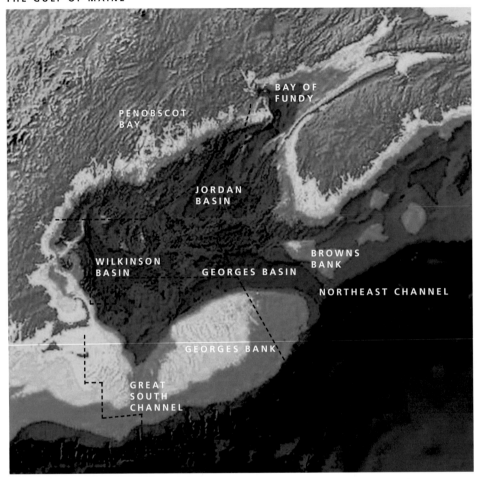

FIGURE 1

The physical structure of the Gulf of Maine creates distinct habitats—based on depth, substrate (bottom type), and water temperature—that affect the distribution and abundance of ground-fish. The government's current management strategy recognizes separate breeding populations of cod, haddock, flounder, and other bottom-dwelling species in four management areas: Gulf of Maine, Eastern and Western Georges Bank, and Southern New England. But emerging scientific evidence suggests that additional populations—not recognized by management—also reside in the inshore Gulf of Maine. Increasingly, fishermen, scientists, and conservationists have argued that if the stocks are to fully recover (and for traditional fishing communities to have access to the resource in the future), a new management boundary must be created to approximate the ecological division between inshore and offshore waters. The red hashmarks represent possible management boundaries that correspond to real ecological divisions. Within the boundary, harvest limits and fishing rules would more accurately reflect local ecological conditions, and fishermen would be required to commit to working exclusively in the area for a set period of time to promote long-term stewardship.
Credit: Bob Stenbeck, University of Maine

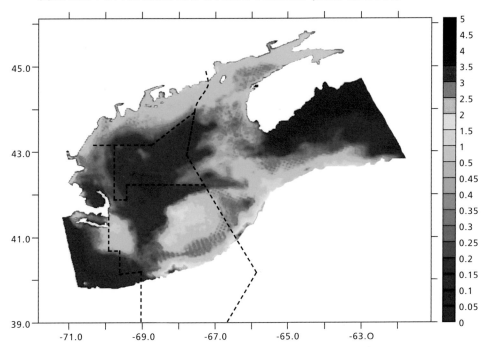

FIGURE 2

A satellite image showing phytoplankton distribution in the Gulf of Maine is graphic evidence of the ecological differences between inshore and offshore habitats. The greatest abundance on the coastal shelf corresponds to the Eastern Maine Coastal Current where tidally mixed water provides high levels of nutrients for groundfish and other organisms.
Credit: Bob Stenbeck, University of Maine

practices, and other cultural and political interests.

Today, the biggest controversy within the industry concerns economic consolidation. Since 2004, after a days-at-sea leasing program was introduced and subjected the fishing privileges to market forces, access to the resource has steadily migrated out of rural ports and into the region's seafood capitals: Portland, Gloucester, and New Bedford.[12] At last count, only 1,000 federal permits remained in the fishery and only one permit is left between Stonington, Maine, on the state's middle coast, and the Canadian border. Even still, NMFS has suggested that the stocks can only support 300 to 500 full-time operations over the long-term. The agency has been less forthcoming about what size vessels and from which ports.[13]

To reduce overcapitalization and end overfishing the government has been seeking to "rationalize" the industry by using a management approach known as individual fishing quotas (IFQs). Under such a system, scientists set a strict harvest limit and then allocate shares (or quota) to qualified fishermen and businesses. The idea is that market forces will reduce the number of vessels, as less efficient operations are bought out by more profitable businesses. The approach can boast

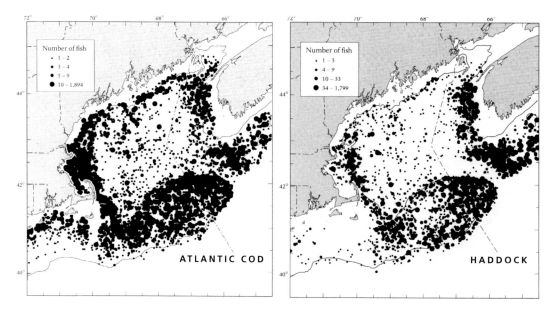

FIGURE 3:
The first three charts indicate aggregate NMFS trawl survey data from 1968 to 1996. The last graphic shows NMFS information combined with more recent assessments (2000-03) conducted by an industry vessel in the coastal waters of Maine and New Hampshire. The evidence illustrates groundfish species' preference for coastal and shallow water habitats and further suggests the need for an additional management boundary inshore.
Credit: Bob Stenbeck, University of Maine

conservation achievements in several fisheries where it has been used around the world, but critics point out that in each of these circumstances, access was also bought up by a handful of corporations, leaving many communities with generations of fishing heritage outside the fishery.[14]

Recent scholarship has shown that policy disputes such as the one described above are rarely just about material interests. In fact, the disagreements frequently reflect conflicting social values that are deeply influenced by historical, cultural, and geographical contexts.[15] A main assertion of this book is that the current New England fisheries management crisis is to a large extent the consequence of one such values debate, about the appropriate balance between the needs of society and the productive capacity of nature. To be sure, the conflict on land has frequently served to sustain the ecological crisis at sea when policies needed to protect fish were stalled or made impotent by politically expedient compromises.

Just to be clear, allow me to reiterate the argument vis-à-vis the role fisheries scientists, the group typically most sensitive to talk of culturally informed values, play in the debate: (1) Objective truths about the marine environment can incontrovertibly be ascertained using the scientific method. (2) The concept of the marine system deployed by NMFS was developed in response to human limitations

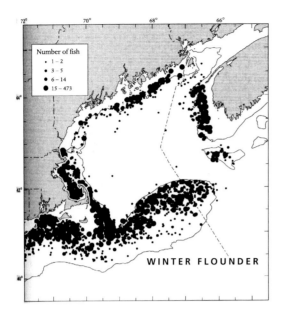

WINTER FLOUNDER

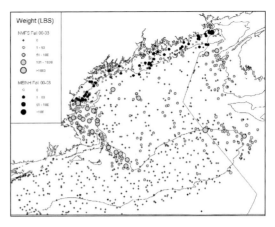

ATLANTIC COD 2000-03
INSHORE AND OFFSHORE

in gathering and processing fisheries data. (3) The protocol is based more on those factors than it is on a reality-based depiction of the system.

Environmentalists come at the problem with their own biases, which are deeply informed by American culture's peculiar history of separating the human and non-human worlds. For their part, fishermen have their own conceptions about their place in the natural world, which is largely predicated on their extensive observations on the water and a need to derive a livelihood from it.

We should not be entirely surprised that the policy debates have turned into such highly charged affairs. For "as soon as we project our values onto the world and begin to assert their primacy by calling them natural, we declare our unwillingness to consider alternative values that in all likelihood are no less compelling for the people who hold them dear," according to historian William Cronon, speaking of the tendency people have to misinterpret social values for objective fact.[16] Common wisdom holds, however, that if there is a solution to the fisheries crisis, the aforementioned stakeholders will have to find some sort of accommodation.

For those readers already made pessimistic by the scale of such an undertaking, there is an upshot to such a theory of culture and conflict. That is, just as we have come to internalize the assumptions about man and sea that underlie our political perspectives, we are able to unlearn them and, better yet, develop new and more socially useful constructions. The purpose of this work is to explore the possibilities for such solutions by examining the experience of the Fleet Visioning Project, a grassroots effort designed to build consensus around the industry's

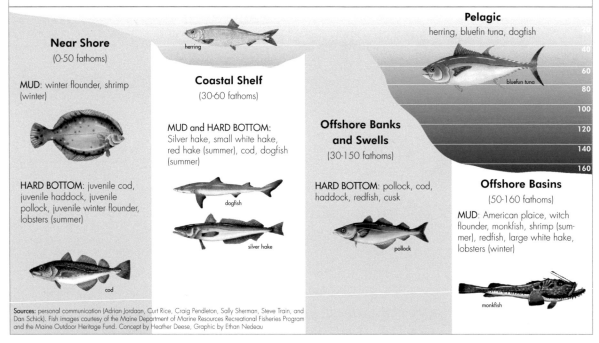

Depth Distributions and Habitat Types for Gulf of Maine Commercial Species

Near Shore
(0-50 fathoms)

MUD: winter flounder, shrimp (winter)

HARD BOTTOM: juvenile cod, juvenile haddock, juvenile pollock, juvenile winter flounder, lobsters (summer)

herring

cod

Coastal Shelf
(30-60 fathoms)

MUD and HARD BOTTOM: Silver hake, small white hake, red hake (summer), cod, dogfish (summer)

dogfish

silver hake

Offshore Banks and Swells
(30-150 fathoms)

HARD BOTTOM: pollock, cod, haddock, redfish, cusk

pollock

Pelagic
herring, bluefin tuna, dogfish

bluefin tuna

Offshore Basins
(50-160 fathoms)

MUD: American plaice, witch flounder, monkfish, shrimp (summer), redfish, large white hake, lobsters (winter)

monkfish

Sources: personal communication (Adrian Jordaan, Curt Rice, Craig Pendleton, Sally Sherman, Steve Train, and Dan Schick). Fish images courtesy of the Maine Department of Marine Resources Recreational Fisheries Program and the Maine Outdoor Heritage Fund. Concept by Heather Deese, Graphic by Ethan Nedeau.

FIGURE 3:
An "ecosystem map" created by fishermen and scientists illustrates how several key species are distributed according to depth in the Gulf of Maine. Some of the best information about the abundance and distribution of New England's fish stocks has come from such fisherman-scientist partnerships.

divergent social goals.

The approach the project took was adapted from many of the insights of humanistic scholarship described above and the work of Paulo Freire, a Brazilian educator and critical theorist. In his seminal work, the *Pedagogy of the Oppressed* (1970), Freire argues that social injustice is inextricably connected to how a society's dominant class conceptualizes the cause of social problems.[17] For instance, if poverty is understood as the consequence of laziness or stupidity, as some contend, then little good could come from trying to help the impoverished out of such a hopeless situation. In practice, his work engaged disenfranchised groups in a conversation about how they believed they came to be poor. The exercise is designed to build awareness about the social and political realities that sustain oppression— knowledge that he believed would help set people free.

An important principle to such a theory, one that is not always fully appreciated but is particularly relevant to the study of groundfish management policy, is that the status quo is very much insulated from change by ideas that are deeply entrenched in our society's collective psychology—even among those of us who profess to be committed to bringing about change. Thus, it is the collective responsibility of social progressives and environmentalists to continually engage in a process of self-reflection, so we can come to see how our thinking and behavior might inadvertently be advancing the same structures of power and exploitation that we seek to change. This undertaking can be a laborious and disorienting task because it demands that we challenge many of the values and ideas that lie at the core of our identity—the essence of who we think we are.

An inconspicuous paperback published in 1980 gets at the heart of confronting the kind of self-awareness I believe is incumbent upon all those who are committed to affecting social change. William Bridges wrote *Transitions: Making Sense of Life's Changes* as he coped with unexpected changes that had severely disrupted his enjoyment of life.[18] The former literature professor argues that understanding the human experience of transition is the first step in making changes we cannot afford to ignore. He describes change as a kind of metaphysical passage that occurs in three distinct phases—an ending, a neutral zone, and a new beginning—a process he calls transition. In other words, transition occurs in the course of attempts at change. It is the state that change puts people into. The *change* is external (the different policy, practice, or structure that the leader is trying to bring about), while *transition* is internal (a psychological reorientation that people have to go through before the change can work).[19]

We stand at a watershed moment in the history of the country's oldest industry. In the past fifteen years we have witnessed the collapse and early recovery of one of the world's most productive biological systems. We have also watched the industry's small-scale independent operations consolidate into a handful of wealthy interests in the name of economic efficiency. But the invisible hand of the market is not the hand of God. Once we identify our present situation as a product of ideas powerfully shaped by our time, place, politics, and culture we recognize how the structures of power and inequality, of which we are part, operate. We begin to challenge the dominant ideology that sustains ecological exploitation and social injustice.

Change is inevitable, as they say. But constructive criticism helps keep changes in line with society's long-term interests and the principles of our democracy. Change, then, is where we should begin.

Ideally, the book's sections should be read continuously. The complexity of the subject matter demands a baseline understanding of terms and concepts that I have tried to gradually introduce over the course of the narrative. Chapter 1 begins by recalling the opening day of U.S. fisheries management in New England in order to introduce the reader to the "commons dilemma" theory. The economic model and its corollaries permeate the history of fisheries management policy and environmental politics. It is suggested that the reliance on the model has ironically served to perpetuate ecologically destructive and socially unjust management. Four of some the most recent academic works on the subject are explored to both introduce the reader to the challenge of fisheries management and to illustrate some of the shortcomings of the analytical tools used by many scholars of the fishery. Whenever possible papers that are accessible online or available in paperback relatively inexpensively were used.

Chapter 2 picks up the story in 1994, when a three-year-old lawsuit brought by environmentalists prompted the strictest fishing regulations to hit the region since foreign fishing was banned in 1977. The narrative then turns upstream to interpret policy change as occurring in two distinct periods. From 1977 to 1994, policymaking largely reflected the council's unwillingness to affirm biological limits, not primarily due to greed but to the fact that such restrictions also require allocating the economic benefits of what remains (a moral decision fraught with political challenges). From 1994 to 2007, after environmentalists applied legal leverage to prevent overfishing, decision-makers grappled with various strategies (and, it is argued, wealthy interests were then able to manipulate the council process to accumulate de facto ownership of fishing access).

Chapter 3 presents the development of the Northwest Atlantic Marine Alliance (NAMA) and its calls for community-based management as part of what social historians refer to as the environmental justice movement. Environmental justice activists differ from mainstream environmentalists who focus primarily on protecting the biodiversity of ecosystems. Instead they argue that some people, especially those who are politically disenfranchised, are also the victims of ecological degradation. Furthermore, they believe some people have found ways to live in ways that are relatively ecologically sound. They advocate for policies that include humans in the solutions to environmental problems.

Chapter 4 pairs the portraits of some of the fishermen, scientists, and environmentalists involved in the community-based management movement with their personal narratives about what motivates them to work toward resolving the fisheries dilemma. These photographs and stories constitute an independently conceived commentary on the fishery, one that complements, in the best sense of the word, the previous text.

NOTES

1. Because numerous species share the same habitat near the seafloor and are often captured by fishermen together they are subject to similar fishing regulations. The species currently included in the Northeast Multispecies management plan are Atlantic cod (*Gadus morhua*), flounder (*Glyptocephalus cynoglossus*), American plaice (*Hippoglossoides platessoides*), yellowtail flounder (*Limanda ferruginea*), haddock (*melanogrammus aeglefinus*), pollock (*Pollachius virens*), winter flounder (*Pleuronnectus americanus*), windowpane flounder (*Scophthalmus aquousus*), Acadian redfish (*Sebastes fasciatus*), white hake (*Urophycis tenuis*), Atlantic halibut (*Hippoglossus hippoglossus*), and ocean pout (*Zoarces americanus*). Soon the same management plan will also include monkfish (*Lophius americanus*) and several skate species due to extensive interactions with other groundfish. For practical reasons each species is managed as two or three homogeneous stocks even though it is widely accepted that they comprise several more geographically and genetically distinct populations.

2. The Fishery Conservation and Management Act Pub. L No. 94-265, 90 Stat. 33 (1976), codified as amended at U.S.C. 1801–1883 (2000), was later renamed the Magnuson-Stevens Act, after its two biggest champions in Congress, Senators Ted Stevens of Alaska and Warren Magnuson of Washington State. When the law was implemented in 1977 it created an Exclusive Economic Zone that made marine resources (oil, minerals, fish, etc.) the public property of American citizens.

3. For an excellent account of the era of foreign factory trawlers see William A. Warner's classic *Distant Water: The Fate of the North Atlantic Fisherman* (Boston: Atlantic–Little, Brown, 1977).

4. Collette, B. B. and G. Klein-MacPhee, (eds.). Bigelow and Schroeder's *Fishes of the Gulf of Maine* (Washington, D.C.: Smithsonian Press, 2002, third edition). A half-century after it was first published the volume is still a key reference for scientists and can be found in the wheelhouse of more than one New England fishing vessel. The Gulf of Maine Research Institute (formerly the Gulf of Maine Aquarium) has published the book and its scientific drawings online: http://www.gma.org/fogm/

5. As recently as September 2007 at a NMFS hearing on the implementation of the reauthorized Magnuson-Stevens Act in Arlington, Virginia, it was obvious that substantial confu-

sion exists between the agency and regional councils about what specific roles and responsibilities they will assume in the enactment phase. Numerous council managers argued that the majority of funding for fisheries management is being allocated to science centers and independent biologists making it difficult for them to adequately implement the new rules. For instance, the New England Fishery Management Council's budget has been flat-lined since 2002 despite significant increases in work and responsibility.

6. For another account of the Amendment 13 controversy and some of the historical context leading up to it see "A Once Great Industry on the Brink," a four-part series in the *Boston Globe* by Beth Daley and Gareth Cook (began on October 26, 2003).

7. See Berkes, et al., "Ecology: Globalization, Roving Bandits, and Marine Resources" iin *Science* (March 2006). Written by leading physical scientists, the paper calls for a restructuring of fisheries management decision-making processes in order to meet the needs of the dynamic ocean environment.

8. My brief description of Gulf of Maine ecology is obviously only a snapshot of the environment, but one that is necessary to understand how it relates to human management strategies. The information is based on interviews with scientists and fishermen who closely study the ecosystem. In particular, Drs. Bob Steneck, Jim Wilson, Les Kaufman, and Yong Chen provided a scientific outlook; while Craig Pendleton, Curt Rice, Proctor Wells, and Bill Lee offered a fishing-based outlook.

9. My general description of NMFS stock assessment protocol is based on a lecture given by Dr. Paul Rago of the New England Fisheries Science Center at the Gulf of Maine Research Institute's "Fish Tank" series and interviews with Drs. Jim Wilson and Les Kaufman. See their September 9, 2003 letter to New England Fishery Management Council chairman: http://www.nescb.org/epub lications/fall2004/kaufman_wilson_main.html

10. The most frequently cited academic paper that argues for the critical importance of understanding the genetic structure of fish stocks when designing management policy is D. Ruzzante, C. Taggart, C. Cook, and S. Goddard's. 1996 "Genetic differentiation between inshore and offshore Atlantic cod (Gadus morhua) off Newfoundland: microsatellite DNA variation and antifreeze level" in *Can. J. Fish. Aquat. Sci.* 53: 634–45. Fisherman and scientist Edward Ames wrote a paper, for which he won a MacArthur Award, that traces historical cod grounds based

on oral histories: "Reconstructing the Gulf of Maine cod spawning grounds on the basis of local ecological knowledge." *Journal of Marine Biological Assessment,* U.K., vol, 80, no, 3675, 1–9.

11. In the winter of 2000 a fisherman noticed that NMFS's primary research vessel used in groundfish stock assessments *(Albatross IV)* was employing faulty fishing equipment. The blunder, which potentially led to fish population estimates lower than actual numbers (and thus lower catch limits than necessary) became a rallying cry for the industry. The event was dubbed "Trawlgate." See "Mistrust between scientists, fishermen mars key mission," by Gareth Cook and Beth Daley in the *Boston Globe,* October 27, 2003.

12. Northeast Multispecies Amendment 13 SEIS, December 18, 2003, 1351. See http://nefmc.org/nemulti/index.html.

13. Both Dr. William Hogarth, director of NOAA Fisheries, and Paul Howard, executive director of the New England Fisheries Management Council, have publicly stated that the fishery can likely only support 300 to 500 full-time vessels long-term.

14. For an objective overview of the use of individual fishing quotas and their impacts on communities around the world see Government Accountability Office Report (GAO-04-277): "Individual Fishing Quotas: Methods for Community Protection and New Entry Require Periodic Evaluation," www.gao.gov/new.items/d04277.pdf

15. The intellectual inspiration for this work can be found in *Uncommon Ground: Rethinking the Human Place in Nature*, published by Norton (1995) and edited by environmental historian William Cronon. The collection of essays approaches the global environmental crisis by recognizing that effective policy solutions must address the role culture plays in shaping the way people treat the natural world.

16. Ibid., 51–52

17. Paulo Freire, *Pedagogy of the Oppressed* (New York: Continuum, 2006).

18. William Bridges, *Transitions: Making Sense of Life's Changes* (New York: Perseus, 2004).

19. Interview with Ken Downes of the Andrus Family Fund, August 2006.

CHAPTER 1

FISHERIES AS THE TRAGEDY OF THE COMMONS

"If they get you asking the wrong questions, they don't have to worry about the answers."
—Thomas Pychon

THE HEART OF THE PROBLEM

"It was like a Shakespearean tragedy," said Robin Alden, founder of *Commercial Fisheries News* and former commissioner of Maine's Department of Marine Resources, when describing the impact fishing quotas had on New England's groundfish industry in 1977.[1]

The rules were designed to safeguard severely depleted groundfish after a decade of heavy fishing by factory trawlers from the Soviet Union, Western Europe, and Japan had driven stocks across the region to the point of collapse; haddock on Georges Bank was so heavily targeted some scientists spoke of the possibility of extinction. It wasn't the first time a quota management system had been used in the Northeast. Prior to the implementation of the Fishery Conservation and Management Act, the fishery was regulated in accordance with the International Commission for Northwest Atlantic Fisheries (ICNAF), a treaty signed by some eighteen nations that utilized the resource in 1970.[2]

The agreement set a total allowable catch and allocated shares to the various fleets, but the communist-bloc vessels, in particular, were notorious for exceeding their allocation. The fisheries act was designed primarily to expel the foreign vessels from U.S. waters. But with an anticipated two-month lag between the day the law took effect, on January 1, 1977, and the time managers needed to design a new management plan, government officials worried that unrestricted fishing would compromise the conservation goals of the legislation so they imposed the quotas on an emergency basis.[3]

Like ICNAF, the stopgap rules set a total allowable catch based on scientific estimates of the stocks' health. NMFS's regional director was given the authority to stop fishing once the limits were met. Importantly, however, there was no element of the plan that guaranteed fishermen access to a profitable share of the catch. On the first of the year the harvest proceeded in earnest. Fearing the season could be closed at any time, fishermen raced their vessels to and from fishing grounds. In a matter of days, seafood exchanges across the region were overwhelmed with landings and prices sank to record lows. By July, just halfway into the season, landings of haddock and yellowtail flounder approached the annual limit; a month later it was announced that cod could only be landed as "bycatch" (a small amount of fish permitted as accidental catch in the haddock, redfish, hake, and a few other fisheries).[4]

With the prospect of the region's most valuable fishery being closed entirely, the New England fishery council convened a series of meetings in early September to "balance the economic impact of closures against the need to conserve and rebuild depleted cod stocks." Following three days of heated debate, the managers agreed to extend the cod harvest, with the understanding that any excesses incurred would be deducted from the allowable catch in 1978. To control the pace of fishing (and account for variable costs associated with the fleet's different scales of operation and gear types), shares of the catch were allocated by vessel class.

For example, vessels larger than 125 gross tons were permitted to land 3,000 pounds of cod per day; those less than 50 gross tons were allowed 2,000 pounds per day. Gillnetters, which anchor their nets to the seafloor for several days at a time, received an allocation of 15,000 pounds per week. Also, offshore vessel owners persuaded the council to grant them an additional three days of fishing to account for "steaming time" to and from fishing grounds.[5]

Because the council worried that allowing landings of cod above the limits would intensify pressure on the stock, the managers imposed a highly controversial measure: fishermen were required to discard any surplus overboard before returning to port. But with their gear plumbing the bottom hundreds of feet below the surface, vessels often could not avoid exceeding arbitrary limits, and it was not uncommon for fishermen to throw several thousands of pounds of dead cod overboard to stay in compliance with the regulations.

Furthermore, the complex system of possession limits created an enforcement nightmare for the Coast Guard, numerous legal loopholes, and widespread violations. By October, most fishermen had lost confidence in the government's ability to manage the fish and the people who depended on them. "Fishermen didn't want to waste fish or break the rules like that," Alden said. "But the system created an untenable situation that undermined a generations-old stewardship ethic and brought out the worst in human nature."[6]

Many readers will recognize the crisis outlined above as reflecting the pattern of exploitation described in Garret Hardin's famous 1968 article, "The Tragedy of the Commons." In the opening paragraphs, the economist recounts a fable about a group of herders who enjoy free access to a common parcel of land. Since they stand to benefit individually by grazing as many cows as possible while the cost to the land is shared by the entire group, there is an incentive for each to add more and more livestock, lest the competition beat him to it. In short order, the soil is exhausted, the pasture fails, and everyone is left worse off.[7]

Hardin's paper actually recapitulates a long-standing theory on the problem of population growth first described by Thomas Malthus in the late eighteenth century. The English clergyman argued that because the human population reproduces exponentially while food can only be grown arithmetically, our species will always be pushing the carrying capacity of available resources and was therefore condemned to a vicious cycle of hunger, disease, and warfare.[8] Different iterations of the theory have emerged periodically ever since, particularly during times of social and political unrest. But coming as it did in the 1960s, a time of intense ecological change and political upheaval, Hardin's article catalyzed a tremendous body of research and profoundly informed America's environmental consciousness.[9]

After Hardin's paper was published, however, numerous scholars, particularly ecologists and humanists, began to raise troubling questions about the hegemony of the commons model. In fact as recently as 1994 some of the country's leading academics from a variety of disciplines assembled on the campus of the University of California in Irvine for a seminar designed to examine how the theory and its corollaries had influenced American environmental thinking. The scholars were concerned that the environmental movement's progress was being hampered by fundamental misconceptions rooted in its intellectual foundation.[10]

"Recent scholarship has clearly demonstrated that the natural world is far more dynamic, far more changeable, and far more entangled with human history than popular beliefs about 'the balance of nature' have typically acknowledged," writes historian William Cronon in the introduction to *Uncommon Ground: Rethinking the Human Place in Nature* (1995, 1996), a volume of essays produced by the seminar. "What happens to environmental politics, environmental ethics, and environmentalism in general once we acknowledge the deeply troubling truth that we can never know at first hand the world 'out there'—the nature we seek to understand and protect—but instead must always encounter that world through the lens of our own ideas and imaginings?"[11] From this starting point, the seminar's participants engaged in lengthy discussions about how the ideas expressed in "The Tragedy of the Commons" and related works could be revised to address the latest insights from ecology, biology, anthropology, history, and other disciplines.

When *Uncommon Ground* was first published it came under heavy criticism by environmentalists who felt it unwittingly supported the argument of the "wise-use" movement, which was in the process of reversing key federal environmental legislation in the mid-1990s. However, a decade of political change has demonstrated that far from supporting anti-environmental causes, the collection speaks to a more progressive and durable variety of environmentalism that engages a wide range of political interests—environmentalists, farmers, ranchers, and fishermen—in the long-term process of conservation.

FIVE DIFFERENT POINTS OF VIEW

In one of the collection's essays, "On the Search for a Root Cause: Essentialist Tendencies in Environmental Discourse," environmental historian Jeffrey Ellis explores the environmental movement's long-standing quest to discover the essential origin of ecological problems. "The logic behind this search for a root cause or causes is compelling. Adequate solutions to a problem cannot be derived or implemented unless those solutions address the problem at its source," he writes.[12] However, because different interpretations of what constitutes the root cause of the environmental crisis—overpopulation, capitalism, technology, and so on—necessarily result in different policy proposals (with different social and political implications), Ellis believes the search formed the center of a heated debate between some of the country's leading environmental intellectuals. Ironically, though the disagreements reflect a shared desire to protect the environment, they have fragmented environmentalists into different factions, ceding valuable political ground to interests like the wise-use movement that is concerned primarily with increased exploitation and the accumulation of wealth.

"The Tragedy of the Commons" surfaced at a time that many consider to be the dawn of the American environmental movement—when the National Environmental Policy Act in 1969 and the implementation of the Endangered Species Act in 1973 provided citizens with the constitutional framework necessary to challenge the perpetrators of environmental degradation. However, Ellis and others have pointed to the limitations of the legal apparatus in addressing the social dimensions of environmental problems or the distribution of social power that is integral to resource exploitation in American life.

The history of fisheries management politics and policies in New England is freighted with this paradox. Another central argument of this work is that deeply embedded within the letter of the Fishery Conservation and Management Act are ideas that have, in fact, prevented groundfish from experiencing a full recovery and have advanced social inequity. Included in those assumptions are the following myths: fishermen are solely responsible for the problem of overfishing; the fishing industry is a homogenous social group; economic consolidation is inevitable in our profit-driven capitalist system. "If we really want to protect fish and fishermen over the long-term we cannot solely rely on an economic model to do it. If so, the real tragedy will be when the fish return, but none of the communities that relied on the resource for over 300 years are able to catch them," says Robin Alden.[13]

To illustrate the argument, let's pick up our ruminations about the fishery in 1960, the year the foreign trawlers first appeared on New England's horizon. It was also the time when the director of the UN's Food and Agriculture Organization's Fisheries Division called on the international fishing industry to expand its operations to stave off global famine. He confidently projected the world's oceans could supply "60,000,000 tons of fish each year without impairing the viability of stocks or drawing on new resources."[14] To be sure, it is not difficult to see how the Malthusian argument influenced the policy recommendation, which appears prominently in many of the operational plans of the Soviet industrial fleet.

Similarly, the main objective of the Fishery Conservation and Management Act was not primarily conservation, as its name implies. In fact, the legislation was designed to ensure the American fishing industry could achieve the optimum economic yield from its coastal waters. Not to be confused with a fishery's maximum sustainable yield—its ultimate biological limit—an optimum yield is the amount of fish that can be extracted without damaging future productivity, "as modified by relevant ecological, economic, and social factors."[15] To that end, the Reagan administration called on some of the country's most respected scientists and administrators in the early 1980s, including Sylvia Earle and John Knauss, to investigate how "the unrealized potential of our marine and coastal fisheries can benefit our Nation."[16]

Chief among the committee's recommendations was an expansion of federal subsidies to the industry to improve its competitive advantage in the global market. "Modern marketing and distribution systems are generally lacking in the

U.S. fishery industry," according to their report. "Modernization of the system would generate increased markets and profits well justifying initial 'seed' assistance from the Federal Government."[17] Today, despite strong evidence showing how eighteenth-century economic models like Hardin's contributed to the collapse of the groundfish stocks, environmentalists and scholars continue to rely on the same paradigm to inform their analysis of the fishery crisis.

One of the most frequently cited works in the expansive literature on the subject is "Ludwig's Ratchet and the Collapse of New England's Groundfish Stocks" (2000), by Timothy Hennessey and Michael Healey.[18] The study is based on a model developed by mathematician Lewis Ludwig that shows how mutually reinforcing economic and political forces work together to drive natural resource systems downward. Based on an exhaustive survey of past environmental crises, Ludwig argues that advances in scientific knowledge and conservation technology have had no meaningful impact on conservation in the face of these compelling social forces. Hennessy and Healey adapt the model for the groundfishery as follows:

1.

Profit or the promise of profit in the fishery attracts political and economic power that, in the face of uncertainty about resource abundance, drives the decision-making process.

2.

Science is unable to measure the abundance of fish accurately enough or to predict future states of the fish stocks well enough to demonstrate the negative effects of over exploitation until it is too late.

3.

In the face of scientific uncertainty, investment in the fishery expands to the point that rents are dissipated and the economic viability of individual fishing units becomes marginal.

4.

When there is a short-term increase in fish abundance, investment in the fishery expands. When there is a short-term decrease in fish abundance, disinvestment is slow and the industry appeals to government for assistance. Assistance is typically given by the government, ostensibly as a short-term measure. In reality, the assistance tends to become incorporated into the functional economics of the fishery.[19]

The study appropriately highlights some of the economic and political forces that conspired to undermine New England's groundfish stocks. As the review indicates, the fishery was the victim of the phenomenon twice, first at the hands of the Communist-bloc fleet, which had its notorious economic inefficiencies offset by the Soviet Union's treasury; and again by a vastly overcapitalized domestic fleet courtesy of the U.S. Department of Commerce. A similar problem persists today in the form of proposals for another round of federally sponsored vessel buyback programs.

But the problem is more complicated than Hennessy and Healey imply. Because changes to fishing rules impact the fleet's various sectors differently, the council not only decides how many fish can be harvested but also who has access to the economic benefits of the resource. For example, in "Taking Stock of the Regional Fisheries Management Councils" (2003), Stanford law professor Josh Eagle, et al, argue convincingly that because it is politically difficult to justify favoring one segment of the fleet over another, the council repeatedly exceeded the total allowable catch recommended by scientists to accommodate the demands of the different interests involved.[20] The failure of Hennessey and Healy to incorporate this component of the groundfish decline not only misrepresents a major motivation behind policy change in the fishery, it also ignores how the same imperatives they describe have been employed by a minority in the industry to accumulate the majority of fishing access.

Furthermore, by defining the problem so narrowly the paper is conspicuously silent on proposed solutions. Presumably, such a frame would argue for a market-based fix, such as individual fishing quotas. By neglecting the moral dimension of the fisheries crisis, however, it makes no meaningful contribution to how the industry's concerns about access can be managed so to expedite the implementation of such a program and conserve fish.

The aforementioned paper by Josh Eagle in some ways picks up where the adaptation of Ludwig's ratchet left off. The legalistic "watchdog" study examined the decision-making process of four regional councils to see if the organizational structure was capable of meeting its legislative imperative to prevent overfishing. The survey revealed that because the councils are not technically part of the federal government, they are exempt from many of the rules designed to ensure objective, transparent, and broad participation in decision-making processes that affect the public interest.[21]

"The regional councils are among the most obscure regulatory bodies in the United States. Although virtually everyone knows that the U.S. Environmental Protection Agency protects the country's air and water quality and that USDA Forest Service manages the country's public forests, few people have ever even heard of the regional councils."[22] The study concluded that as currently structured the councils are unlikely to resolve the problem of overfishing and identified four main reasons why:

1.

The councils decide both how many fish can be caught and who can catch them. Because larger catches are easier to divide up among competing fishery interests, the councils' responsibility to allocate catches encourages them to set lax fishery limits, undermining conservation.

2.

More than 80 percent of the citizens who are appointed to the councils by the Secretary of Commerce represent the fishing industry. Homogeneous groups are less likely to produce well-considered decisions than groups with diverse membership.

3.

The large number of council members drawn from industry results in ubiquitous conflicts of interest. Yet the conflict of interest rules that apply to the councils are very weak compared to those that apply to other government decision-makers.

4.

Despite its legal responsibility to carefully oversee the councils, NMFS gives them significant leeway in decision-making.[23]

The paper goes on to propose actions that NMFS and Congress can take to promote better conservation in the nation's fisheries. First, it calls on the agency to tighten conflict of interest policies for the councils. Today, members are only required to recuse themselves from voting when they own or represent more than ten percent of the affected gear type or sector. "A lower threshold would reduce the most direct conflicts of interest."[24] Second, it suggests the Secretary of Commerce improve the diversity of interests represented on the councils by encouraging state governors to submit a broader list of candidates through their power of approval authority. Finally, it proposes that NMFS limit the discretion it gives to councils in setting catch limits by having its science centers and stock assessment panels make more specific harvest limit recommendations.

The paper, which is frequently cited by environmental attorneys in challenges to council decisions, is one of the most comprehensive analyses of the organizational impediments to sustainable fisheries. It does not call for the removal of commercial fishermen from councils, as some radical conservationists have suggested. In fact, it recognizes the importance of having decision-makers familiar with local ecology and fishing practices be part of the fishery management process. However, by focusing on how the design of the system fails to ensure the conservation of *fish* it completely ignores whether or not the same framework is adequate to ensure a fair distribution of access to the diverse groups of *fishermen* that make up the industry. Nor does it deal with how conflicting expectations between fishermen have slowed the adoption of strict harvest limits and other conservation measures as the council and elected officials battle over the social implications of the policies.

By far the most naïve and problematic of the recent literature on the fishery is "Fish Stories: Science, Advocacy, and Policy Change in New England Fishery Management" (2006) by Judith Layzer, an assistant professor of environmental policy at the Massachusetts Institute of Technology.[25] The paper begins by taking the opposite view of Eagle, describing the fishery as "a conservation success" story. It flatly dismisses the influence "well-funded" interests have had on policymaking either to the detriment of the fish or other members of the industry. (Remarkably, Layzer also downplays the role material interests have had on any American policy debates, which is akin to arguing that the pharmaceutical and petroleum lobbies have no meaningful impact on the development of the policies that regulate their respective industries!)

The paper does provide a valuable pedagogical service by laying out two prevalent conceptions of policy change in the author's field, what she calls the "rational-comprehensive" and "material-interest-based" models. The first interprets policy evolution as the product of a kind of rational-scientific measurement of the relevant problem. Under this lens, policy analysts are seen to research a particular topic and consult experts about the root source of the problem. Based on this assessment, various solutions are proposed, with the one seen as most beneficial to society finally being selected. The later model interprets policy change as a response of the government to the influence of powerful interest groups.[26]

Layzer finds both of the approaches unable to explain how more restrictive "risk averse" policies were adopted by the council beginning in 1994. Alternatively, she argues that the environmental lobby (itself a "well-funded" interest) persevered because it was able to deploy a more persuasive political narrative about the problem of overfishing. "Two factors were critical to the environmentalists' success: a compelling and credible scientific story about the relationship between fishing and the health of fish stocks, and an explicit conservation requirement in the language governing fishery management," according to Layzer.[27]

First, we'll need to grant the professor a measure of charity as to what constitutes a "success" in fisheries management. It is true that the region's stocks have experienced a substantial rebound since the regulations with which the paper is concerned went into effect. However, with the exception of haddock and several other species, most of the stocks in the multi-species complex are expected to fall below or just barely make the biological targets called for by the same rules when the government releases its biological assessment in August 2008. What's more, most scientists attribute the bumper haddock crop to the excessive removal of the species' main competition from the ecosystem.

It is also important to recognize the recovery she identifies has not been uniform across the region. In fact, because the fishery is made up of several geographically isolated stocks, the communities adjacent to these ecosystems, on the central and eastern Maine coast for example, have not benefited from the increase in haddock and cod found in the western part of the ocean. The distinction is important, not only so the public is accurately informed about the status of its marine resources, but also to help assess whether the economic benefits of the resource are being distributed fairly.

For the balance of the article, the professor cites episodes of civil disobedience by fishermen in response to increasingly strict regulations as reported in the news media. Her lack of appreciation for the political and historical contexts of the protests, however, is rather astonishing for someone in her profession. For instance, she illustrates how NMFS repeatedly bought into the industry's "risk tolerant" definition of the problem and allowed overfishing by quoting a federal judge who ridiculed the agency's "floundering oversight." Then, a few sentences later, she undermines her argument by describing how a rowdy "armada of fishing vessels from New Bedford, Gloucester, Provincetown, Chatham, and other New England ports jammed Boston Harbor to protest the new rules" that forced the fishermen to live within limits.[28] She ignores the idea that the fishermen might have been protesting the same incompetence described by the judge, much as the poor and other minorities might demonstrate against their lack of access to heath care and education afforded by our government.

By considering the historical context and using the tools of responsible scholarship, it is possible to see the demonstrations in a different light. The emotional turmoil prompted by policy changes is as much a part of the fishery's story as foreign trawlers, the Magnuson Act, and the increasingly stringent regulations that followed.[29]

Indeed, is not difficult to identify with those angry fishermen: At the time of the cuts your business has high overhead costs. You know that maintenance, fuel, ice, dockage, and other expenses will quickly mount without a steady stream of revenue. Just a few years before, the government had encouraged you to expand by offering subsidies so, maybe, you have a $200,000 mortgage to contend with as well. Now, the government that told you to catch more fish says you catch too many and, because of its mistake, you had to take a 50 percent pay cut. But your anger runs deeper than frustration over lost wages and government incompetence. You think about growing up in a family and community where fishing is all you know. As a kid you loved the kind of freedom you felt only on the water and you want your children to have the same opportunity if they choose it. The fishing life is rough and dangerous, yes, but with hard work it can support a family and maybe send your kids to college. For you, fishing is what makes sense of the world, it is the foundation of your identity, and it is suddenly under attack by bureaucrats and environmentalists who don't know their port from starboard.

To conclude this review, let's consider a highly original paper that helps summarize the hazards associated with focusing on only one element of environmental problems that are most certainly multi-causal in origin. "Re-Placing the Space of Community: A Story of Cultural Politics, Policies, and Fisheries Management" (2005) was written by Julia Olson, one of the few anthropologists employed by NMFS to assess the social impacts of fishing regulations.[30]

The paper draws on the author's frustration with trying to communicate the products of her research to an agency dominated by a rigid bio-economic view of the resource and fishing communities. The effect, she argues, is the "tendency to look at communities as places that get impacted...plays down their context and histories and brackets anthropology to the description of impacts. This loses those more proactive senses of communities that stress what communities can do rather than what is done to them, and renders less visible the multiplicities of interests, positions, and values in any given community."[31]

To illustrate her argument, Olson reflects on some of the language deployed in the congressional debates that helped shaped the Sustainable Fisheries Act, which updated the Magnuson–Stevens Act (an amended version of the Fishery Conservation and Management Act) in 1996. The law institutionalized concerns about the social impacts regulations have on fishing communities by defining the term, and requiring managers to "take into account the importance of fishery resources to fishing communities."[32] The rhetoric is particularly rich for such an analysis because it occurred at time of heightened controversy in U.S. fisheries management.

In 1995, for example, large habitat closures designed to protect inshore cod off the coast of New England displaced hundreds of small-scale fishing operations. At the same time, on the Pacific Coast, tension was building between a large corporate-owned factory fleet from Seattle and small fishing ports in rural Alaska over control of a valuable segment of the region's salmon fishery. "It was the debate about onshore and offshore processors, and the small and large-scale," Olson writes. "That powerfully brought up the question of who was a real fisher and thus what was a real fishing community."[33]

Initially, senators from Alaska and Massachusetts suggested the statute define fishing communities as places "substantially dependent on the *harvest* of fishery resources to meet social and economic needs" (italics added). But a delegation from Washington State strongly objected to the wording, believing it prejudicial to mobile fishing operations that processed fish in the North Pacific.

Eventually the meaning of fishing community adopted by lawyers at NMFS came to include fishing vessels that process fish far from their homeports as well as rural localities dependent on harvesting resources. This final interpretation "had the ironic effect of standardizing the local and implying that only economics really matters after all," according to Olson. "This construction of community as an empty space serves again to erase social differences."[34]

NOTES

1. Interview with author, June 2006.

2. Warner, 7–8.

3. David E. Pierce, "Development and Evolution of Fishery Management Plans for Cod, Haddock, and Yellowtail Flounder" (1982: 1). On file at the New England Fishery Management Council.

4. Ibid., 4–9.

5. Ibid., 10–11.

6. Interview with author, March 2006.

7. Garrett Hardin, "The Tragedy of the Commons," *Science*, 162: 1243–48, (1968); see http://dieoff.org/page95.htm8. Thomas Malthus, *An Essay on the Principle of Population*. Available online at http://www.ac.wwu.edu/~stephan/malthus/malthus.0.html9. On the impact Malthus's and Hardin's theories have had on the contemporary environmental movement see Jeffery Ellis's "On the Search for a Root Cause: Essentialist Tendencies in Environmental Discourse" in *Uncommon Ground*, 256–68.10. See William Cronon's introduction to *Uncommon Ground*, 23–56.

11. Ibid., 25.

12. Ibid., 257.

13. Interview with author, June 2006.

14. Warner, 87.

15. Quoted in Josh Eagle et al, "Taking Stock of the Regional Fishery Management Councils" (Pew: 2003, 14). See http://fisheries.stanford.edu/Stanford_Council_Report.pdf

16. "Fisheries for the Future: Restructuring the Government-Industry Partnership: National Ocean Goals and Objectives for the 1980s" in preface. (National Advisory Committee on Oceans and Atmosphere: July 1982, quoted in introduction) on file at Bowdoin College.

17. Ibid, preface.

18. T. Hennessey and M. Healey, "Ludwig's Ratchet and the Collapse of New England Groundfish Stocks," *Coastal Management* 28: 187–213, (2000).

19. Ibid., 189.

20. See Eagle.

21 Ibid., 4.

22. Ibid., 5.

23. Ibid., 5.

24. Ibid., 34.

25. Judith Layzer. "Fish Stories: Science, Advocacy, and Policy Change in New England Fishery Management." (*Policy Studies Journal*, 34: 1, (2006).

26. Ibid., 60.

27. Ibid., 59.

28. Ibid., 72.

29. This hypothetical depiction is based on narratives told by several fishermen during Fleet Visioning Project meetings.

30. Julia Olson, "Re-Placing the Space of Community: A Story of Cultural Politics, Policies, and Fisheries Management," *Anthropological Quarterly*, Winter 2005, 247–68).

31. Ibid., 249.

32. Ibid., 251.

33. Ibid., 251.

34. Ibid., 255.

CHAPTER 2

ATTEMPTS AT REGULATION

"We will argue about these things forever, and the arguments will not vanish just because we appeal to nature to defend our case. But if we listen closely, we human beings can learn a great deal from the tales we tell of such a place. This silent rock, this nature about which we argue so much, is also among the most important things we have in common. That is why we care so much about it. It is, paradoxically, the uncommon ground we cannot help but share." —William Cronon

THE LAW OF UNINTENDED CONSEQUENCES

"We started out trying to resolve the dilemma and soon found ourselves caught in the middle of it," said Peter Shelley, vice president of the Conservation Law Foundation (CLF) and lead attorney on the lawsuit that led to the adoption of days-at-sea management.[1]

In the decade leading up to the legal action, even as New England's groundfish fleet doubled in size and landings soared to record levels, CLF and the region's other environmental organizations had largely ignored the issue. It seems almost incomprehensible today, considering the fishery's highly partisan climate, but before the lawsuit Shelley and CLF worked closely with the fishing industry to oppose offshore oil drilling and advocate for strict clean water standards. In fact, it wasn't until some of these allies, mostly inshore fishermen, brought the groundfish crisis to Shelley's attention in the late 1980s that CLF began to investigate the problem. "Fishermen are one of the best sources of information about the health of the marine environment. Their livelihoods depend on having a close understanding of ecology, so when something changes they notice," said Shelley.[2]

Beginning in 1982, when managers voted to abandon quota management after it led to derby fishing and atrocious regulatory discards, they initiated a system of indirect controls to regulate the harvest: gear restrictions, habitat closures, and special access programs. The strategy helped slow the race to fish and reduced the waste; however, nearly every season thereafter management plans were submitted and approved by NMFS that led to landings far in excess of the ocean's maximum sustainable yield.

As early as 1984 indications that an ecological catastrophe was underway reached shore after fish exchanges in the storied ports of Gloucester and Boston experienced their worst seasons on record. At the same time, fishermen from across the region found that they had to steam farther and farther from shore to stock enough landings to cover the cost of gas. "The writing was on the wall pretty early," said Proctor Wells, who still fishes out of Phippsburg, Maine, a small community situated on the shore of the New Meadows River. "Us inshore guys didn't have the size or horsepower to steam all over creation looking for fish. So when the fleet in southern New England began to catch all the fish before they migrated north we were in a world of trouble."[3]

Wells and other inshore fishermen repeatedly raised their concerns at council meetings, but said managers were primarily concerned with maintaining the industry's revenue at levels that could support the big capital investments of the 1980s. Shelley attended his first council meeting in 1987 at the urging of fishermen. "It was immediately obvious that the council system was inherently flawed. The decision-making process was structured in a way that was detrimental to the biological system and fishermen who didn't have enough power to influence policy," he said.

In fact, marine biologists at the Northeast Regional Science Center had been sounding the alarm about the dangers of overfishing since 1977. Regulations were implemented in a way, though, that made scientists powerless over how their information fed into policy. Dr. Vaughn Anthony, who was NMFS's chief scientist at the regional office during some of the fishery's most controversial periods, in the 1980s and 1990s, described the pitfalls of the governance structure by email in 2007:

> The Council members seldom *ever* seriously doubted our assessments, but simply and repeatedly said that their management would depend more on fishermen's needs rather than a rebuilding process and "F" (fish mortality) levels. I didn't have a problem with this, but I could not change it, they were the managers and we clearly were not! They knew that the stocks were in trouble but decided not to restrict the fishing because the fishermen continually said they would go out of business under further restrictions… It wasn't a case of ignorance on their part as to the status of the stocks but rather what they decided to do about it. The scientists never were part of the management process and, in fact, we were ordered to stay out of it.[4]

To be sure, in 1987, frustrated with the council's unwillingness to address the ecological crisis building off the region's shores, scientists convinced NMFS officials to use the agency's authority to refine the interpretation of "overfishing" in the Magnuson-Stevens Act.

The new language, known as the 602 guidelines, found that if excessive fishing was occurring a program must "be established for rebuilding the stock over a period of time specified by the Council and acceptable to the Secretary."[5] In 1989, barely a decade after the government took control of the industry in order to save it, the new standard for overfishing forced the council to acknowledge that the fishery was on the verge of collapse. Nevertheless, the managers still failed to design the rules necessary to begin a recovery. On May 31, 1991, in Amendment 4—its next scheduled change to the groundfish plan—NMFS clearly violated the 602 guidelines.

The following month, CLF and the Massachusetts Audubon Society filed suit against the Department of Commerce, NMFS, and the agency's regional office for failing to prevent overfishing on three stocks. Notably, the council was not named as a defendant in the case because the plaintiffs did not believe the Magnuson–Stevens Act intended the body to be a "responsible party" in failing to enforce limits.

It was a cut-and-dry case. The judge quickly found for the plaintiffs on all counts and ordered the parties to immediately design the regulations necessary to remedy the situation. Industry representatives repeatedly petitioned to be included in the negotiations, but were denied. "A lot of the bad blood between the industry and environmentalists can be traced back to us getting cut out of those discussions," said Craig Pendleton, an outspoken draggerman from Saco, Maine. "We weren't trying to subvert the process, we wanted to fix it. We were cut out of the talks and it was a real blow to our confidence in the process."[6]

The new rules, known as Amendment 5, were made public the next year. To achieve the 50 percent reduction to fishing effort that scientists believed was necessary for the stocks to rebuild, the strategy proposed cutting the time fishermen were allowed to fish by 10 percent a year over the next five years (previously, vessels spent anywhere from 180 to 300 days a season at sea). The rationale behind the strategy was to control fishing mortality in a way that avoided dangerous derby fishing and negative market consequences, by giving fishermen the flexibility to work when weather and prices were most amenable.[7] But the plan's failure to set a strict harvest limit in line with the regenerative capacity of the ocean reflects the central dilemma of multi-species management in the context of scarcity: risk continued overfishing with flexible catch limits or face the moral and political challenges of allocating shares of a total allowable catch.

Notwithstanding, Amendment 5 could not avoid allocation entirely. After all, the fishery's total days-at-sea were roughly linked to the number of fish scientists believed could be safely extracted from the ocean. Furthermore, the managers were forced to devise a system that determined what share of the total "fleet days" each vessel would be granted. The inshore fleet argued that the fleet days should be distributed equally to all federal permit holders; the offshore fleet, however, said such an allocation was insufficient to cover high overhead costs and successfully lobbied for a distribution based on evidence of recorded fishing time.

Considering the political and legal demands put on the managers, Amendment 5 was a good faith effort to control fishing in a relatively fair way, but it suffered from major flaws that undermined its success. For instance, neither the council nor NMFS maintained accurate records about the fleet's fishing capacity at the time. Lacking a better alternative, the government established a crude correlation between recorded business expenditures in the 1989, 1990, and 1991 fishing seasons and total fishing effort. "We were asked to produce settlement sheets, fuel, grocery, and ice receipts, records of repair work, almost anything that could be roughly construed as proof of days at sea," said Pendleton.[8] In one story, emblematic of the program's shortcomings, a vessel from New Bedford reportedly produced evidence for fishing 400 days in one remarkable season.

Moreover, the days-at-sea system was predicated on questionable assumptions: First, it assumed a one-to-one ratio between fishing effort and fishing mortality, a misapprehension that failed to recognize how technological advancements in gear and electronics improved the fleet's killing power annually. Second, the strategy treated the daily fishing mortality inflicted by a 100-foot dragger as equivalent to that of a 40-foot vessel. Third, the system was blind to the ecological realities of groundfish and the corresponding behavior of the fleet. That is, fish move about the ocean to eat, reproduce, and congregate when and where they find an abundance of food and shelter. Fishermen closely studied these patterns for generations and passed the knowledge on by word of mouth or in a captain's treasured logbook. To be most effective, regulations should have addressed how, when, and where fishing occurred rather than flatly cutting effort.

The concerns outlined in the CLF complaint wound through the fisheries bureaucracy for three years before they were addressed by a policy change. By that time, stock assessments indicated that a 60- to 70-percent reduction to the cod harvest in both management areas (not 50 percent as initially assumed) would be necessary to allow stocks to rebuild.[9] It was also determined that even bigger cuts would be necessary to revive haddock and flounder populations. "We repeatedly warned NMFS, the council, and environmentalists that the approach created negative conservation incentives and was likely going to make the problem worse. No one would listen," said Pendleton.[10]

On May 1, 1994, the day Amendment 5 was implemented, inshore and offshore vessels lined the inshore Gulf of Maine from Provincetown to Port Clyde, as Pendleton and his colleagues had predicted. "No one in their right mind is going to burn up a day-at-sea steaming offshore when they can make money right off the beach," he said.[11]

The same month, a sixth amendment was hastily developed to protect the severely depleted haddock on Georges Bank. The action pushed hundreds more vessels, which previously worked in southern New England, into the Gulf of Maine. Curt Rice, who was running a trawler out of Portland at the time, remembers the impact. "Before Amendment 5, the inshore and offshore fleets had pretty much been separated. It made sense: big vessels operate on high volume and have the size to get offshore," he went on. "But they need to make a living like everyone else, so when we went on the clock [offshore vessels] moved inshore. I remember looking at all those boats, thinking that cod weren't going to last long under the pressure."[12]

1977–1994: AVOIDANCE OF AN ALLOCATION

Mark Simonitsch, a fisherman from Cape Cod who retired after more than thirty years of fishing and as the owner of a commercial pier in 2006, remembers the psychological impact of the Fishery Conservation and Management Act back in 1977. He said that with the foreign fleet gone and millions of dollars of subsidies pouring into the region's dilapidated waterfronts, a kind of irrational exuberance settled in. "We thought that our time had come…people were dancing in the streets. No one imagined what was to become of the fishery that had provided for us for so long."[13]

Even before the legislation was implemented, the Department of Commerce had initiated a number of economic development programs to help the domestic fleet improve its efficiency. In the late 1970s and early 1980s the Capital Construction Fund, the Fisheries Obligation and Guarantee Program, and a handful of other federal programs financed the construction or recondition of 291 fishing vessels in the Northeast, at a cost of approximately $128 million to taxpayers.[14] It is estimated that the productivity of the fleet increased by 10 percent annually during the period. The impact on the ocean was incontrovertible: Georges Bank cod landings soared from nearly 15,000 to 39,000 metric tons (that's enough fish for 60 million table servings) between 1977 and 1982.[15]

In addition to vastly improving the industry's efficiency, federal management also prompted a number of fishing behaviors antithetical to conservation. For example, possession limits in theory designed to minimize fishing mortality in practice resulted in unthinkable waste. "There was a horrific amount of discards," recalls Jim O'Malley, who was fishing out of Rhode Island in the late 1970s. "It seemed like for every 500 pounds of flounder we caught we had to dump 1,000 pounds of haddock overboard. This was *required* mind you, but it sure as hell didn't save fish." During the quota period an untold number of fish (perhaps in the tens of millions of pounds) were discarded. "It's a crime against nature to waste fish like that, but that's what the system did," O'Malley said.[16]

The increasing complexity of the early quota system made enforcement futile. "It was impossible to figure out who was in compliance and who was in violation because of the web of exemptions," said Tom Nies, who was a Coast Guard boarding official in the late 1970s. "We were virtually powerless to provide effective oversight."[17] Furthermore, lax prosecution of violators further undermined the industry's confidence in the process. In early October 1977, for example, the council sent a frantic telegram to the Secretary of Commerce:

> Administrative delays by the federal government in the prosecution of violations of domestic fishing regulations established under PL 96-245, Fishery Conservation and Management Act, have caused serious social, economic and biological problems within the New England fishing industry. The government's failure to prosecute quickly and effectively appears to condone violations to the detriment of the living marine resources and to law-abiding fishermen.[18]

While the council waited for a response, it convened NMFS scientists to quantify the ecological impact of the management problems that first season. The news was sobering: the haddock quota had been exceeded by 89 percent, Gulf of Maine cod by 110 percent, and western yellowtail flounder by 28 percent. Consequently, it was recommended that there be no directed fishing on Gulf of Maine cod in 1978; that Georges Bank and southern cod harvests be reduced by 50 percent; and haddock and yellowtail across the region be held to bycatch only.

"There was a justifiable concern that once total 1977 catch (cod as well as haddock) was determined and NMFS groundfish survey results were known [and] by the time Plan modifications could legally be in place (March 1977) catch might have approached or even surpassed the entire allowable 1978 harvest," David Pierce, a council staff member at the time, wrote in a meticulous internal review of the quota management period at its conclusion in 1982.[19]

Based on the poor stock assessment information, the council quickly drafted a compromised set of limits and sent it to NMFS for approval. On November 3, 1977, the secretary of commerce agreed to the plan; however, the managers were astonished to learn that the regulations signed into law differed substantially from the ones they had submitted. Specifically, the additional landings the council recommended for cod were also extended to haddock and yellowtail, and the weekly limit for gillnetters was increased to 16,000 pounds per week for each species. "After a wait of approximately six weeks to discover the status of its recommendations," wrote Pierce. "Council members were polled by phone by the Regional Office of NMFS to determine if the Council would approve these alternative recommendations. A two-hour deadline was given for a decision and reportedly it was a 'take it or leave it' offer."[20]

On November 16 the council's groundfish committee met informally to discuss amending the quota management system to address overfishing and the excessive discards. But "as it was discovered [NMFS's] recommendations had to be decided on and submitted to the secretary of commerce the next day in order to meet a timetable for emergency implementation on January 1, 1978." With just hours to fix the catastrophic failures of the previous year, and without the benefit of staff consultation, the committee recommended extending the optimal yields set by NMFS into 1978 (to be revised later based on current stock assessments, gear research, and the most recent landings data.) Additionally, the managers suggested replacing annual catch limits with a quarterly system in an attempt to extend the harvest further into the year.[21]

The next week, the director of NMFS met with the council to explain the unorthodox policy changes. He attributed the move to the legal ramifications of violating the Fishery Conservation and Management Act's maximum sustainable yield provision. "Since it was 'illegal' to take more than OY [optimal yield], but it was evident that cod and haddock OYs had been surpassed and yellowtail catches were approaching OY, a definite option was to shut down the fisheries for these species entirely," Pierce wrote of the director's reasoning. Thus, to avoid closing the fishery, NMFS was bound to raise the optimal yield on cod. "It was felt that changes for one species could not legally be defended without including the others,"[22] so the limits on haddock and yellowtail were increased as well. In other words, to justify overfishing NMFS simply redefined the meaning of overfishing.

The next time the full council met, in early December, great attention was given to the committee's proposed rules and the manner in which they were developed. Council members, representatives from NMFS, and the fishermen in attendance disagreed deeply about the proposed limits for 1978. Some insisted the restrictions were too harsh. Others believed that the council needed to "bite the bullet" and enforce the strict limits in order for stocks to recover. In the waning hours of the night on the second day of heated debate, Frank O'Hara, a groundfish committee spokesperson, made a motion to set limits for the first three months of the year at one-quarter of the 1977 annual quota. In short order, the motion passed and the meeting was adjourned, ending debate and leaving fishermen stunned.[23]

A January 1978 article in *Maine Commercial Fisheries* (which later became *Commercial Fisheries News*) described the event:

> To say that fishermen were upset and angry at the way the Council handled the evening session is the grossest of understatements. Fishermen predicted economic disaster and threatened to blockade harbors. They were somewhat mollified when Mr. Peterson (the Director of the Massachusetts Division of Marine Fisheries) pointed out that the quarterly quota would make more fish available than had been caught during the same period in 1977, but there was still the feeling that things were getting worse, not better, under the 200-mile legislation.[24]

The fishermen's confidence in management eroded further that month when the agency made another surprise revelation: Reversing its November action, the government unilaterally closed all fishing on December 20, stating in a press release: "It was not feasible to extend the November 3 emergency regulations (45-day duration) for the remainder of the year, since harvest projections indicate that the quotas would be further exceeded."[25]

On January 1, 1978, the season's hastily devised management plan was implemented on a temporary basis. The industry was invited to propose alternative plans "intended to spread allowable harvest through the fishing seasons in order to prevent a fisheries closure and to provide all vessels with reasonable access to and share of the harvest" to be used in the 1979 season. To that end, the council embraced the principles of a plan submitted by the Massachusetts Inshore Draggermen's Association and the Cape Cod Fishermen's Coalition.[26]

The strategy recognized that many of the past management problems were related to the uncertainty created by having a total allowable catch without individual allocations. To correct the problem, the industry-based plan allocated a portion of the harvest based on evidence of historical landings. However, though the plan was an improvement over the quota system, it did not prevent vessels from fishing one area to depletion before moving on to the next. Furthermore, the plan did not create accountability for the consequences of overfishing. At the time, the Coast Guard was too overwhelmed to provide adequate enforcement. The rules also failed to establish incentives that promoted stewardship by fishermen. Not surprisingly, the violations continued: some draggers were outfitted with gill nets in order to claim two allotments; other captains fiddled with departure and arrival times and changed their homeport registrations to gain access to more fish; highly mobile fishermen simply moved from place to place.[27]

On June 28, 1978, NOAA's administrator wrote a prescient letter to the New England Council's chairman to express his concerns about the fishery's future:

> As with any fishery in which there are too few fish and large numbers of fishermen with high expectations, effective management will require hard choices. For instance, it may be necessary to consider seriously a moratorium on new entry into certain heavily exploited fisheries. It will be necessary to allocate among small boats and large boats, commercial and recreational fishermen, and so on. We are committed to assist the Council in making those decisions and to foster the conservation of the resources, in compliance with the Act.[28]

However, rather than making the "hard choices" necessary to change the status quo, the council and NMFS balked, choosing instead to stiffen trip limits, gear restrictions, and other indirect controls. Stocks continued to spiral downward.

With no end to the ecological and social crises in sight, Allen Peterson, a council member from Massachusetts, suggested a new direction. He argued that the web of rules, discards, and violations made it impossible to ascertain which management tools had worked and which had failed. He thus urged the council to reset the fishery's optimum yields to zero, explaining that he was "not so naïve to believe that the threats of closures will not [disappear] once the council's plan is implemented in total even with quarterly OYs beginning anew, but at least we will be able to fairly judge the plan on its merits."[29] After several months of debate the council and agency agreed and the fishing season effectively began again on October 1, 1978.

Whatever the wisdom of Peterson's idea it at least gave the managers an opportunity to focus on developing a long-term management system, to be known as the Atlantic Demersal Finfish Plan (ADFP). The relatively progressive approach began by calling for a moratorium on "additional vessels from having access to species under regulation."[30] Limiting entry to the fishery was (and remains) one of the most controversial management measures because it upsets the ability for young fishermen to enter the trade. Additionally, rumors about the forthcoming moratorium triggered a rush on permits, which increased by 50 percent between 1977 and 1978.[31]

Development of the ADFP underscored one of management's biggest shortcomings at the time: managers did not maintain accurate records about the number of vessels that were active in the fishery. To ameliorate the problem, NMFS recommended that a voluntary data reporting system be implemented in 1979. The council argued any such system had to be mandatory. "The crux of the problem was confidentiality," wrote Pierce. "It was feared by many that unless fishermen could be absolutely assured that their catch data could never be accessed and traced back to them (as individuals), industry cooperation in providing accurate information would diminish and the integrity of catch data used to perform biological assessments would suffer."[32] After battling with officials at NMFS for months a mandatory system was finally approved. Nevertheless, stock assessments from the time showed that several stocks were in imminent danger.

Fearing a total biological collapse, Spencer Apollonio, the council's groundfish committee chairman, made a motion at an August 1979 meeting to abandon species quotas, vessel class allocations, trip limits, and seasonal and geographical allocations as soon as possible. It was hoped that his plan would provide some basic conservation measures for protection of the stocks during the interim period prior to the development of a more comprehensive ADFP and provide proper environments for acquisition of data and council policy decisions necessary for ADFP development," Pierce wrote. "The [Apollinio] Plan was considered by many to be a new approach to management and a better alternative to the current Plan which has led to problems for which there are no solutions, issues which cannot be resolved, and an environment in which even the most rationale measures are not accepted.'"[33]

The council's interim plan was quickly dubbed "open fishing," because it abandoned the strict harvest limits under the quota system. The term is somewhat of a misnomer, though, because the interim plan also imposed the most restrictive gear limitations up to that time and closed large swaths of prime fishing habitat despite rigorous objections by some members of the industry. What's more, most inshore fishermen opposed the system because they believed it would quickly lead to increased landings and low prices, and put them at a competitive disadvantage to vessels with large operational scales. "You'll need a big vessel now to go after the poundage," William Halsen of Weymouth, Massachusetts, told a *Boston Globe* reporter in 1982.[34]

The plan initially slowed the pace of fishing largely because it made the fleet less efficient, but it also invited new problems. For example, operations that targeted squid, redfish, whiting, hake, and other species that require small mesh complained that the new gear restrictions were economically untenable. Consequently, a special area was established on Georges Bank that allowed the vessels to tow $5^{1}/_{8}$-inch mesh when the rest of the fleet was required to use $5^{1}/_{2}$-inch twine.[35]

The habitat closures also raised questions of fairness. "We had a terrible time justifying the closures. Fish are not distributed fairly throughout the ocean, so protecting habitats impacted the ports closest to the closures most and caused tremendous resentment," said Robin Alden, who served on the council at the time.[36] The managers spent the next two years refining the proposal to accommodate various aspects of the fleet, but the Coast Guard concluded that the final conservation benefits did not justify the $16 million the revised plan would cost to enforce.[37]

In the summer of 1984, landings at the region's key ports bottomed out: cod fell by nearly 3,000 metric tons, haddock were down 1,000 metric tons, and yellowtail plummeted by 6,000 metric tons. The situation seemed likely to deteriorate that fall when the World Court awarded Canada control of the Northeast Peak, 9,000 square miles of prime fishing grounds on Georges Bank, effectively pushing dozens more American vessels into the Gulf of Maine.[38] Scientists at NMFS ramped up their warnings. Dr. Vaughn Anthony wrote:

> From 1980 or so to about 1984 we (scientists) stayed away from the Council meetings. Later, I worked very closely with the Council to develop how we provided assessments to them, both in time and in standardized figures, tables, and reports that they could understand (little scientific jargon

and regular reviews).... They knew that the stocks were in trouble but decided not to restrict the fishing because the fishermen continually said they would go out of business under further restrictions. The Council procedure was based on the hope that we might get a good year class next year and the problems would be over.[39]

Even as the evidence of an impending collapse became impossible to deny, powerful fishing interests were still able to influence congressional delegates.

For example, in August 1987, New England senators Cohen, Mitchell, Kennedy, Kerry, Chafee, and Pell sent a letter to the secretary of commerce urging him to consider the social and economic impacts of restrictions proposed to slow the decline.[40] "There was little advantage, really, for politicians to publicly support the science," said Anthony. "To say how wonderful the fishermen were and that—they were only trying to make a living—produced more votes. I always understood this. Science is science. It needs no outside help, other than funding. The Council made the decisions and the politicians helped them continue to allow overfishing."[41]

In the early 1990s, following the lead of CLF, a number of national environmental groups turned their attention to the groundfish problem in New England and the nation's other public fisheries. The biggest effort came from the Marine Fish Conservation Network, an alliance of more than a hundred environmental and conservation-focused fishing groups headquartered in Washington, D.C. In 1992, the group began to call for a major revision of the Fishery Conservation and Management Act (known by that time as the Magnuson–Stevens Act after its biggest champions in the Senate, Warren Magnuson of Washington State and Ted Stevens of Alaska).

Ever since the legislation was enacted over exploitation was permitted to occur in more than a third of the country's fisheries, largely due to the statute's ambiguous language regarding a stock's optimum yield, which several councils had used repeatedly to justify harvests in excess of a stock's maximum sustainable yield. From 1992 to 1996, the network coordinated an intense media and lobbying campaign. The district's airwaves and billboards were bombarded with advertisements warning about the dangers of overfishing and lobbyists descended on Capitol Hill and recited the New England groundfish story as evidence of the need to amend the fisheries law. Today, more than a decade later, veteran congressional staffers still recall many details of the groundfish crisis that they learned during the campaign. To be sure, the proposed changes were so fundamental that the reauthorized bill was given a new name: the Sustainable Fisheries Act (SFA).

Initially, it appeared that the effort might face stiff opposition from a Republican-controlled Congress, which was in the midst of reversing key environmental legislation at the time. But a twist of fate allowed its proponents to move forward. The rollback of environmental laws, which were portrayed as putting the interests of obscure species like owls and salamanders ahead of job creation, threatened to hurt moderate Republicans from the Northeast who represented more environmentally sensitive constituents than landlocked conservatives. The SFA thus provided a measure of political cover and Representative Wayne Gilchrest of Maryland was able to muster bipartisan support as the bill's sponsor.

With wide bipartisan support, the amended law changed the definition of "optimum yield," from the amount of fish that could be safely harvested from a fishery "*as modified* by any relevant economic, social, or ecological factor" to the amount of fish that "is prescribed on the basis of the maximum sustainable yield from the fishery, *as reduced* by any relevant social, economic, or ecological factor." The reauthorized law also directed managers to set especially strict limits for overfished stocks and all fishery management plans were required to "establish a standardized reporting methodology to assess the amount and type of bycatch occurring in the fishery and include conservation and management measures" to reduce avoidable waste. Finally, it compelled managers to identify essential fish habitat (EFH) and take action to minimize the impact fishing gear had on the nursery grounds and spawning areas.[42]

As Congress worked out the details of the act, New England's groundfish were reeling under changes in fishing effort caused by the days-at-sea system. Given the choice between using up their limited fishing time steaming offshore, hundreds of large vessels began targeting inshore groundfish stocks, which hit their lowest levels on record in the mid-1990s. In 1995, facing yet another collapse, NMFS imposed 9,000 square miles of "rolling closures," seasonal protections designed to coincide with cod spawning periods in the coastal waters. "For me, the closures were an acknowledgment by the government that they had screwed up. Years before, we explained the need to protect spawning biomass, and warned that days-at-sea would hurt inshore stocks," said Pendleton. "A year later, after the damage had been done, the government finally acted."[43]

Fishermen's attitudes about the closures largely fell along geographic lines. The New Bedford and Gloucester fleets (situated on the front end and middle of the cod's migration route) generally opposed the rules. But, farther north, fishermen supported the measure. "Maine's inshore fleet, in a sense, is a prisoner to ecology. We need a steady stream of fish to come to us. If southern New England gets them first we lose," said Curt Rice, who now captains the fishery's industry-based stock assessment survey. "As much as they hurt, in my mind, the rolling closures and closing Jeffery's Ledge were among some of the first rules that made any sense."[44]

By 1995, it was clear beyond any reasonable doubt that the country's oldest fishery was in serious trouble. Stock assessments indicated severe depletions of groundfish stocks across the region. Fishermen, meanwhile, had begun to put off maintenance and go to sea shorthanded to make up for the ensuing drop in revenues. Still, that fall, as the council considered new adjustments to the fishery management plan in light of the deteriorating situation at sea and on the waterfront, Maine Senator William Cohen sent a letter to the council asking for "a better balance between the need to set a goal to replenish stocks in a timely fashion and the need to maintain a viable industry throughout the recovery period." Representative James Longley, Jr., also from Maine, echoed his colleague in separate letter: "Make some modifications if you must, but do not destroy Maine's groundfishing industry solely to accomplish recovery rates faster."[45]

Proctor Wells recalls being conflicted about his personal financial needs and the ecological needs of the fishery at the time. "It was an impossible situation. By that time (1995) we started to recognize that catch history was going to be the standard for access in the future…even though we knew the best thing for the fish was for the council to make the hard cuts, the big guys were still pushing for more…. With future access tied directly to how many fish we killed, we had no choice but to go along with it."[46]

Mark Simonitsch remembers the anguish he saw on the faces of his friends at the council meetings that year. "The mid-1990s marked a psychological turning point for the inshore fleet. By that time the guys had done a lot of soul searching and were committed to making the changes necessary to save the fishery, but the system wouldn't allow it. In fact, it punished them for conserving. It was an awful feeling." Simonitsch remembers the words of Dr. Vaughn Anthony at a council meeting in 1995, which for him perfectly summarized the state of the fishery at the time. Anthony had told the crowd of fishermen, "Events have overcome us."[47]

By the time politicians took up the SFA debate in Congress, representatives from national corporate fishing interests and even some environmental groups had begun to push for the privatization of the nation's marine resources. Although the groups had different agendas they shared the same basic strategy. In short, proponents of market-based fisheries management plans interpret overfishing as a problem of ownership. Like the herders in Garret Hardin's commons fable, there is no incentive for individuals to conserve for the future because no one in particular owns the resources.

Under the privatized approach—most prominently individual transferable quota (ITQ) systems—regional councils set a strict allowable catch in line with a stock's maximum sustainable yield, and allocate a privilege to harvest a portion (known as a quota) to qualified fishermen, vessels, and corporations. Participants can then fish, lease, sell, or otherwise transfer their quota according to program guidelines and federal regulations. The rules give managers greater control of overfishing and are intended to reduce fishing capacity as fishermen in financial trouble sell their quota to more profitable operations.[48]

New Zealand set up an ITQ system in 1986. Several other nations with depleted stocks also implemented this system. New Zealand's fishery slowly recovered under quota management; today 80 percent of its stocks are rebuilt. However, the experience highlighted a major drawback of privatization. Within just a few years, quotas rapidly migrated from the mom-and-pop operations in rural ports and to corporations in a few urban centers. Today, four corporations control 72 percent of the access to New Zealand's fisheries.[49]

In 1990, NMFS began experimenting with IFQs in the Alaskan halibut and black cod, the South Atlantic snapper-grouper, and the Mid-Atlantic surf clam/ocean quahog fisheries. But in light of the New Zealand example and concerns expressed by constituents, Congress turned a critical eye to market-based fisheries management. For example, shortly after the ITQ programs were implemented in U.S. fisheries, a House report criticized NMFS for "forcing" regional councils to privatize and added that the systems have the potential "to fundamentally alter fisheries management in the U.S." Furthermore, Senator Ted Stevens of Alaska, the namesake of the country's principal fisheries legislation, proposed that the Sustainable Fisheries Act be used to suspend all ITQ programs until NMFS had more adequately investigated the potential negative social impacts of the strategy.

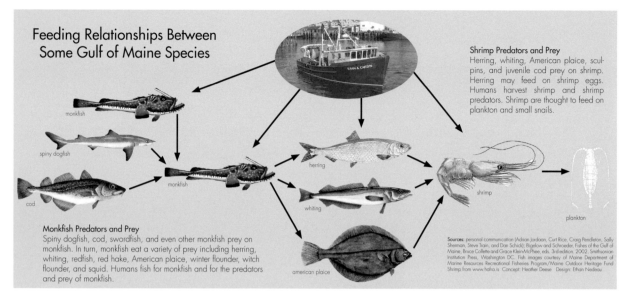

Feeding Relationships Between Some Gulf of Maine Species

Shrimp Predators and Prey
Herring, whiting, American plaice, sculpins, and juvenile cod prey on shrimp. Herring may feed on shrimp eggs. Humans harvest shrimp and shrimp predators. Shrimp are thought to feed on plankton and small snails.

monkfish

spiny dogfish

cod

monkfish

herring

whiting

shrimp

plankton

american plaice

Monkfish Predators and Prey
Spiny dogfish, cod, swordfish, and even other monkfish prey on monkfish. In turn, monkfish eat a variety of prey including herring, whiting, redfish, red hake, American plaice, winter flounder, witch flounder, and squid. Humans fish for monkfish and for the predators and prey of monkfish.

Sources: personal communication (Adrian Jordaan, Curt Rice, Craig Pendleton, Sally Sherman, Steve Train, and Dan Schick); Bigelow and Schroeder, Fishes of the Gulf of Maine, Bruce Collette and Grace Klein-McPhee, eds. 3rd edition. 2002. Smithsonian Institution Press, Washington DC. Fish images courtesy of Maine Department of Marine Resources Recreational Fisheries Program/Maine Outdoor Heritage Fund Shrimp from www.hafra.is Concept: Heather Deese Design: Ethan Nedeau

FIGURE 5:
Another ecosystem map created by fishermen and scientists illustrates the numerous interdependencies between predators and prey. Many fishermen, scientists, and conservationists have expressed concern that, for management to be effective, stock assessment science must reflect how ecological relationships have an impact on the abundance of commercially valuable species (what is known as ecosystem-based management).

It also raised ecological concerns. The Marine Fish Conservation Network worried that the systems led to highgrading, where low-value fish are discarded in favor of a more profitable catch. The conservationists also feared that stock assessment science wasn't reliable enough to ensure that the set harvests matched the biological productivity of the ocean. Additionally, they argued that the strategy's reliance on single-species management contradicted emerging evidence that indicated the need to apply a more holistic, ecosystem-based approach to fisheries management. In 1998 NMFS finally adopted a version of the SFA that included a moratorium on the creation of new quota programs through 2000.

In 1999, on the heels of the revision of the Magnuson–Stevens Act, the Senate scheduled a series of public hearings to respond to catastrophic management failures in several stocks on both coasts and their constituents' concerns about economic consolidation. At one of the meetings, Maine Senator Olympia Snowe did not conceal her frustration with NMFS as she questioned Penelope Dalton, the agency's assistant administrator at the time:

Ms. Dalton, let's go back to the original issue—which goes to the heart of a number of the problems we are facing, not only in the implementation of

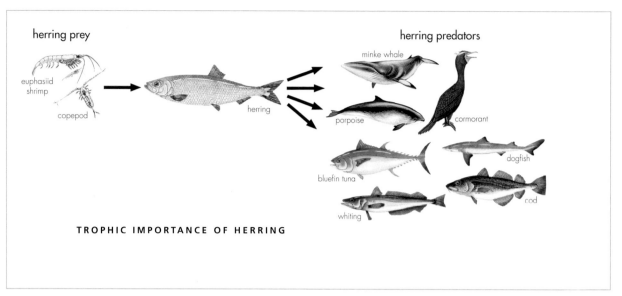

TROPHIC IMPORTANCE OF HERRING

FIGURE 6:
This ecosystem map created by fishermen and scientists illustrates how the health of numerous predators such as groundfish, marine mammals, and seabirds is closely tied to the abundance and availability of Atlantic herring. Recent studies suggest that the depletion of herring in coastal waters may be having an impact on the health of groundfish and other predators in the inshore Gulf of Maine

the Act, but also the intent—of building trust and credibility between an agency, Congress, and more importantly, the people who have to live by the rules, regulations, and legislation. For example, the fact that the agency failed to notify an important segment, on an issue that has been an unprecedented agreement between commercial and recreational fishermen to accept closures in an area, is really remarkable. To not consult, or even inform, the relevant industries is a betrayal of trust between an agency and the people it affects most directly.[50]

Senators from Alaska, Texas, Mississippi, Massachusetts, and other coastal states expressed similar frustrations.

Later, concerns about the social impacts of quota management became a principal part of the conversation. For example, when asked about the risks of quota management, Richard Lauber, chairman of the North Pacific Management Council—which began using IFQs in 1990—shared a precautionary tale:

A person who supports IFQs reminds me of a friend of mine who had a beautiful Cape Hatteras boat, with twin 671 diesel engines in it, and he asked me and my wife to go out one evening to roast some hamburgers in a cove, and so we did, and this boat would send up a wake that made the Alaska ferry system look like it was a row boat, and he was merrily, on a beautiful evening on a flying bridge, sailing along and passing by fishing boats and small craft and so forth, looking straight ahead and having a wonderful time, and meanwhile I am looking back and people are hanging on and banging around, and he is swamping boats and so forth. I liken that to IFQs. As long as you just look ahead and say, look, this is making our management easier, and it is wonderful and so forth—IFQs are wonderful, but if you ever look back at the people that you have ruined, you are not proud of that.[51]

Curiously, around the same time, Republican Senator Stevens, who originally advocated for the limit on the use of IFQs, reversed his position, saying that his concerns about their social impacts had been addressed. Similarly, in spite of strong opposition from a majority of fishermen in his state, Democratic Senator John Kerry of Massachusetts came out in favor of lifting the quota moratorium. He also argued that standards could be put in place to prevent excessive consolidation. "Congress should not continue to punt on the issue of quota-based management," said Kerry. "Why should fishermen in the Gulf of Mexico and the Pacific Northwest be forced to participate in dangerous derby fisheries simply because Congress is afraid to tackle this difficult issue?"[52]

As support for IFQs gained momentum, members of Maine's fishing communities began to travel to Washington to urge their leaders to extend the ban. "We wanted to let them know our concerns," said Reverend Ted Hoskins, from Stonington, Maine. "Over time transferable quota tends to migrate into fewer hands. In bad years, small holders sell off quota—not in great wisdom, but in great need." Barbara Stevenson, who owned a number of offshore boats in Portland at the time, agreed with Hoskin's analysis in the same article, adding, "ITQs would destroy downeast Maine."[53]

The next year, Senator Snowe joined forces with her colleague John McCain of Arizona, who though representing a landlocked state was philosophically opposed to the tendency quota systems had of creating monopolies. The two legislators co-sponsored the "IFQ Act of 2001," which proposed extending the ban on ITQs for another three years. Notwithstanding, in the face of mounting support for privatization by the agency, members of Congress, and several national environmental groups, the moratorium was allowed to expire.

With the ban lifted, Stevens—chair of the senate's powerful appropriations committee—further advanced ITQs by inserting a rider into the 2004 spending bill that created a processor quota (IPQs) system in Alaska's crab fishery. The rider, which was introduced late at night in the final hours of debate over the bill, substantially altered national quota guidelines by allowing seafood processors (rather than only fishermen) to purchase shares. The plan forced Bering Sea crab fishermen to sell 90 percent of their catch to twelve specified corporations (five of which are foreign owned as well as interests represented by Stevens's son who was a lobbyist at the time), leading many fishermen to complain that it turned them into sharecroppers. The rider also upset McCain, who said that it created "fisheries cartels." Snowe argued that it complicated her efforts to find a compromise that would allow a national quota program to move forward.[54]

The controversy further indicated that Congress was far from the kind of consensus necessary to pass the next scheduled update to the Magnuson–Stevens Act. In 2003, the Bush Administration, ideologically in favor of privatizing a number of sectors in the country's economy, announced its intent to expand ITQs nationally. The declaration prompted the Marine Fish Conservation Network and other opponents of market-based management schemes to prepare for another political battle. They found support from Representatives Tom Allen of Maine and William Delahunt of Massachusetts, who had watched with concern when the quasi-private days-at-sea leasing system approach led to consolidation in their home fisheries. Allen and Delahunt co-sponsored "The National Quota Standards Act of 2005." The bill recognized the tremendous political momentum enjoyed by quota supporters and strategically sought to protect mom-and-pop fishing operations from consolidation if an ITQ system became unavoidable. The legislation proposed restricting the amount of quota one individual or corporation could hold; setting aside shares so young fishermen could attain access if the cost of quotas became astronomical, as was the case in other ITQ fisheries around the world. It also called for two-thirds majority referendum vote by the industry before any IFQs could be introduced in New England. Finally, it proposed a sunset provision to ensure that the system was meeting its ecological and social goals.

As Congress approached the midterm elections in November 2006, most fisheries analysts were skeptical that the Magnuson–Stevens Act, much less the quota standards bill, would be voted on before the end of the year. However, Senator Stevens indicated a strong desire to revise the law before the end of the session and struck a compromise with Senator Snowe and other delegates on language that carried relatively robust environmental protections and limited the scope of ITQs in New England. However, substantial distance still separated the Senate compromise from the House's bill, with a number of Representatives still unwilling to support additional quota standards—either because they saw them as superfluous to regulations in Magnuson–Stevens or contrary to the interests of their constituents.[55]

Following the Democratic sweep that November, the balance of power in Congress tilted toward proponents of quota standards. Representative Allen seized the opportunity to broker bipartisan support for an en bloc amendment that provided safeguards for mom-and-pop operators and rural fishing ports. Near midnight, in literally the final minutes of the 109th congressional session, the Magnuson–Stevens Act was reauthorized. "Inclusion of these amendments in the final bill assures that small operations, especially family owned boats and fleets, will have access to their fair share of the resource and won't be swept aside by the massive industrial fishing juggernauts," said Allen. The action "ensures that decisions about fisheries management policy will take local concerns fully into account and provide for local voices to be heard in the management decision-making process."[56]

In terms of conservation, the reauthorized bill took an additional step toward keeping harvests under a stock's maximum sustainable yield by requiring councils to be "accountable" for overages. However, just as with the New England council so many times before, Congress was unable to reach consensus on language that clearly prohibited overfishing. According to congressional aides who worked on the negotiations, the compromise foundered on disagreements over what was meant by "accountability." Rather than further stalling the reauthorization, the politicians agreed to allow NMFS lawyers and the regional councils work out the final details.

Today, common wisdom seems to indicate that the standard adopted will require councils to set hard TACs (total allowable catch) or make up for any excesses in the subsequent fishing year. In the late summer of 2007, the agency made a public request for comments on the development of Limited Access Privilege Programs or LAPPS, in essence a modified quota-based management strategy. Most veterans of the New England fishery policy debate believe this strategy makes some form of market-based management all but certain by the 2010 fishing year. The council and stakeholders must decide how such a program would be structured and thus what impact it would have on the character of fleet in the future.[57]

NOTES

1. Interview with author, March 2006.
2. Ibid.
3. Interview with author, May 2006.
4. Interview with author by email, April 2007.
5. Quoted in Layzer, 70.
6. Interview with author, May 2006.
7. Peter Shelly et al, "The New England fisheries crisis: What have we learned?" *Tulane Environmental Law Journal,* (1996), 229).
8. Interview with author, May 2006.
9. Shelley, 230.
10. Interview with author, May 2006.
11. Ibid.
12. Interview with author, July 2007.
13. Interview with author, June 2006.
14. Federal Fisheries Investment Task Force report to Congress, July 1999. (On file at New England Fishery Management Council, 89).
15. Collette, B. B. and G. Klein-MacPhee, (eds.), Bigelow and Schroeder's *Fishes of the Gulf of Maine.*
16. Interview with author, January 2007.
17. Interview with author, April 2007.
18. Quoted in Pierce, 16.
19. Pierce, 17.
20. Ibid., 18.
21. Ibid., 19.
22. Ibid., 19.
23. Ibid., 22.
24. Ibid., 22.
25. Ibid., 22.
26. Ibid., 25
27. Tom Nies, interview with author and Pierce's paper, 47.
28. Quoted in Pierce, 41.
29. Quoted in Pierce, 37.
30. Pierce, 53.
31. Pierce, 18.
32. Ibid., 105.
33. Quoted in Pierce, 62-63.
34. Article included in Pierce's paper.
35. T. Hennessey and M. Healy, 199.
36. Interview with author, January 2007.
37. T. Hennessey and M. Healy, 200.
38. Layzer, 68.
39. Interview by email, April 2007.
40. Shelley,
41. Interview with author by email, April 2007.
42. Roger Fleming, et al, "Twenty-Eight Years and Counting: Can the Magnuson-Stevens Act Deliver on Its Promise?" *Vermont Law Review,* (Spring 2008), 585–89.
43. Interview with author, March 2007.
44. Interview with author, July 2007.

45. Quoted in Layzer, 73.

46. Interview with author, June 2006.

47. Interview with author, June 2006.

48. See GAO report for an overview of privatized fisheries management: Individual Fishing Quotas: Management Costs Varied and Were not Recovered as Required. March 2005. See http://www.gao.gov/new.items/d05241.pdf

49. Leith Duncan, "In Search of Fish and Chips," *Samudra*, (March 2003), 11.

50. Transcript from 1999 Reauthorization of the Magnuson–Stevens Fishery Conservation and Management Act field hearing. December 14, 1999. (Washington: U.S. Government Printing Office, 44).

51. Transcript of oversight hearing: "Implementation of the 1996 Amendments to the Magnuson-Stevens Act," July 22, 1999. US House of Representatives–Subcommittee on Fisheries Conservation, Wildlife, and Oceans. Washington, D.C.:Government Printing Office._

52. Quoted in *Fishermen's Voice,* September 2000.

53. Ibid.

54. J. R. Pegg, "Fish Conservation Overridden in Final Omnibus Spending Bill," *Environment News Service*, January 23, 2004.

55. Interview with congressional staff, March 2007.

56. "Maine Congressman successfully leads effort to protect the interests of small, family owned fishing operations." Press Release December 7, 2006.

57. Congressional staff said that allocation and accountability were the most contentious issues during reauthorization negotiations and nearly derailed the effort. It is likely that by remaining relatively vague the intent was to allow for the regional councils to hash out the local differences that characterize the eight regions.

CHAPTER 3

THE ENVIRONMENTAL JUSTICE MOVEMENT

"The special human mark, the special record of human passage, that distinguishes man from all other species...is rare enough among men, impossible to any other form of life. It is simply the deliberate chosen refusal to make any marks at all.... We are the most dangerous species of life on the planet, and every other species, even earth itself, has cause to fear our power to exterminate. But we are also the only species which, when it chooses to do so, will go to great effort to save what it might destroy." —Wallace Stegner

DEVELOPMENT OF A NEW KIND OF POLITICAL ALLIANCE

In June 1995, a year after days-at-sea management took effect in New England's groundfishery, Dee Hock, founder of Visa Credit Card International, met with Craig Pendleton to discuss the severe socioeconomic impacts the regulations were having on the region's inshore fleet and fishing communities. It may seem an unusual pair, a banker and draggerman, to be contemplating the intricacies of fisheries management, but, it turns out, Hock is no ordinary banker and Pendleton no ordinary fisherman.

Visa's ex-officio had come to Portsmouth, New Hampshire, to meet with a group of fishermen, scientists, and conservationists at the invitation of the Conservation Law Foundation (CLF). It had been a year since the organization's lawsuit prompted the region's toughest fishing regulations since the foreign fleet was expelled in 1977, but the results had not exactly been what the environmentalists intended: cod mortality was way up in the inshore fishery and to make matters worse hundreds of small inshore operations—the vessels with the least impact on the ocean—were the hardest hit by the rules. "CLF recognized pretty early on that we had fought the wrong battle [with Amendment 4]," said Peter Shelley, lead attorney on the lawsuit. "The management system was so broken it needed to be totally reevaluated, from the ground up, if we were to find a solution that was capable of protecting fish and fishermen."[1]

In early 1995, Doug Foy, the former president of CLF, asked Shelley to look into an innovative management approach that Hock had been lecturing about on the West Coast. After retiring from the credit card business, the banker began to explore how Visa's unorthodox business model could be adapted for the management of complex ecological and social dilemmas. The revised plan, known as "Chaordic" (a synthesis of chaos and order), grew out of a branch of chaos theory and Hock's experience with international finance. Both of these sources showed that the linear functions employed by conventional economics and business management—seen in the geometric political boundaries of the American West and the downward flow of corporate power—were insufficient to account for the realities of ordinary life: jagged coastlines, swirling ocean currents, the ebb and flow of money in the electronic age. The world, in short, is more complex than we know—or maybe more than we can ever know. "Hock convinced me that if there was a solution to the fisheries management crisis it was going to look much different than the government's current approach," said Shelley.[2]

When Hock sat down to ponder the challenges facing the credit card industry in the early 1970s, he began by deconstructing the plans—right down to core principles and basic assumptions—that had repeatedly tried and failed to expand the industry across the country and around the globe. He believed that by relying on some of the most cherished values of capitalism and business management, including vertically integrated "top-down" decision-making and relentless competition, the models failed to effectively manage the new realities of the industry: thousands of diverse cultures, languages, political philosophies, currencies, and legal systems worldwide.

The crux of the problem, as he saw it, was a paradox inherent to the business culture: On one hand, the world's financial institutions engage in intense competition (they issue their own cards and pursue the same customers). But for an integrated system to work the same competitors must cooperate (cards must be accepted by banks in every corner of the earth). Hock's proposed solution was radical only in its simplicity: make no changes to the diverse practices of the world's financial infrastructure, but realign incentives in such a way to encourage cooperation in the necessary fields of activity.

Put simply, for a bank to participate in the Visa network it must agree to basic principles of practice (an agreement indicated by the familiar icon printed on the lower right-hand corner of the network's cards). It must also participate in the organization's computer-based clearinghouse operation, which carries out timely transactions, payments, and billing. Otherwise, members are free to make decisions, such as pricing and marketing strategies, in accordance with the demands of their locality.[3]

Craig Pendleton, a fisherman who had sat on the board of a local credit union for years, immediately saw the relevance of Hock's approach for the fisheries crisis. "Like the early credit card models, NMFS was taking a command and control approach to fix a problem so complex it could only be effectively managed at the local level," he said.[4] Others saw promise in the model and agreed to meet periodically over the next year to discuss the matter further, traveling to Hock's house in Half Moon Bay, California, on several occasions to get counsel firsthand.

From the beginning, Hock asked the group to strip the fisheries management dilemma down to its most basic components. "We kept on coming back to the same issues: NMFS was too far removed to effectively manage the biological and social complexities of the fishery," said Jennifer Atkinson, another CLF lawyer involved in the meetings. "Therefore the alternative solution we imagined was a decentralized governance structure that relied on fishermen's local knowledge and engaged them in the day-to-day management process."[5] Like Hock, Atkinson and her colleagues had to resolve a stubborn paradox. In the name of saving fish, their solution advocated giving greater decision-making power to people with a motivation to kill as many fish as possible.

The banker insisted that it was possible to align the industry's self interest in a way that promoted both the ecological and the social good. Over the following months, the group continued to meet and each time narrowed the focus of the discussions to the basic values that inspired their work. "I was repeatedly surprised to see how profoundly committed fishermen were to conservation strategies," said Shelley. "I think that the management failure and controversy surrounding the crisis created unfair stereotypes and obscured the sophisticated understanding of marine ecology and stewardship shared by many fishermen."[6] After several of these dialogues, which at times resembled "an Alcoholics Anonymous meeting," (and with Hock acting as a kind of spiritual guru), the group finally settled on a mission statement that encompassed their shared values for the fishery: "To restore and enhance an enduring northwest Atlantic marine system, which supports a healthy diversity and abundance of marine life and human uses."

The group then developed a blueprint for a non-profit organization capable of putting the ideas into action. Like Visa, the Northwest Atlantic Marine Alliance (NAMA), as it came to be called, parted company with its industry peers, which typically had only represented single fishing interests—trawlers, gillnetters, hook fishermen, and so on—opening membership to any individual or group that agreed to following principles of practice:

Each and every part of NAMA shall:

1.

Be open to all individuals and institutions that fully subscribe to the purpose and principles.

2.

Have the right to organize in any manner, at any scale, in any area, and around any issue or activity, which is relevant to and consistent with the purpose and principles.

3.

Vest authority in and make decisions at the most local level that includes all relevant and affected parties.

4.

Surrender only such autonomy and resources as are essential to the pursuit of the purpose and principles.

5.

Have an equitable opportunity and responsibility to participate in discussions and deliberations.

6.

Deliberate and make decisions by methods and bodies that represent a full diversity of views and interests and are not controlled by any single view or interest.

7.

Deliberate and make decisions using current and objective knowledge and information derived from scientific methods and practical experience.

8.

Have an equitable obligation to provide knowledge and information that is relevant and essential to the realization of the purpose and principles and that is collected in a way that has minimal impact on confidentiality and competitive position.

9.

Maintain the highest standards of credibility and ethical conduct, fair and accurate dissemination of information, and full disclosure and accountability for its affairs.[7]

Pendleton was named NAMA's first coordinating director and, to ensure a commitment to a diversity of interests, its bylaws required the organization's board

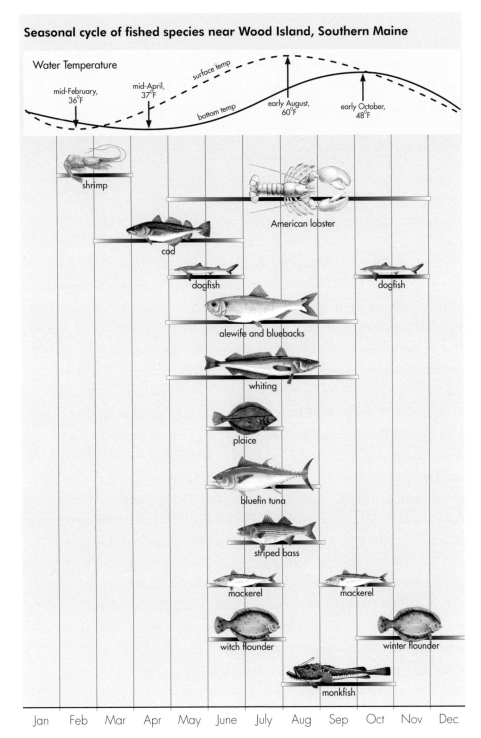

Seasonal cycle of fished species near Wood Island, Southern Maine

Water Temperature

surface temp

mid-February, 36°F

mid-April, 37°F

bottom temp

early August, 60°F

early October, 48°F

shrimp

American lobster

cod

dogfish

dogfish

alewife and bluebacks

whiting

plaice

bluefin tuna

striped bass

mackerel

mackerel

witch flounder

winter flounder

monkfish

Jan Feb Mar Apr May June July Aug Sep Oct Nov Dec

FIGURE 7:
This map demonstrates the seasonal distribution of commercially valuable species in the Gulf of Maine. The region's inshore fleet once harvested numerous species throughout the year, much as a farmer would rotate his crops, to take advantage of fish when they were abundant without putting too much pressure on any one stock. However, the practice declined as access to the groundfishery increasingly became determined by catch history, which created an incentive for fishermen to focus heavily on cod, haddock, and flounder or risk losing their permit.

of trustees to represent a diversity of fishing interests. Shelley, who many in the industry (including Pendleton), had demonized for his role in the lawsuit, was appointed the first chairman.

OVERFISHING AND INJUSTICE

The purpose of this essay is to present the development of NAMA and its efforts to promote community-based management as part of what social historians call the environmental justice movement. The movement is generally traced to 1982, when a group of predominately poor African American women protested the dumping of toxic waste in a Warren County, North Carolina, landfill. Environmental justice activists, in contrast to mainstream environmentalists, advocate for policies that recognize local communities as valuable problem-solvers in natural resource dilemmas. They argue, "some humans, especially the poor, are also the victims of environmental destruction and pollution and that, furthermore, some human cultures live in ways that are relatively sound ecologically," according to feminist scholar Giovanna Di Chiro.[8]

In terms of the groundfishery, environmental justice activists believe the long-term sustainability of the ecosystem demands a close partnership between scientists, managers, and fishermen: the actual people who derive a livelihood from the sea. The campaign's most vocal adherents are typically independent small-scale fishermen from rural ports. The movement has also attracted supporters from the scientific and conservation communities, who believe eliminating fishermen from policy decision-making process is practically irresponsible and politically naïve.

New England's inshore fleet, which is predominantly characterized by small owner-operated vessels from rural ports, was particularly vulnerable to the socio-economic impacts of the regulatory changes in the 1990s for a variety of reasons. First, scientific evidence strongly suggests that the region's coastal fishing grounds are home to genetically distinct sub-populations of groundfish. The stocks' relatively small numbers and geographic isolation, such as an the inshore population of cod that resides east of Penobscot Bay, makes them less resilient to fishing pressure than the large "meta-stocks" recognized by the government, which replenish fishing grounds throughout the Gulf of Maine during annual migrations in the spring and fall. Consequently, the inshore fleet's traditional fishing grounds have not experienced the same rebuilding as the stocks west of Cape Ann and on Georges Bank.[9]

Second, the fleet's scale of operations limits its mobility and harvesting capacity. Such restraints serve as a valuable conservation tool, but when the council allocated fishing privileges based on the highest recorded landings (the bigger the catch, the more days-at-sea allocated) small vessels received a relatively modest share or were eliminated entirely.[10] What's more, some of the fishery's most important spawning habitat is located inshore. Consequently, rules designed to protect essential fish habitat disproportionately impact the small dayboat fleet's grounds. While large vessels are able to steam hundreds of miles offshore in search of fish, inshore boats have been relegated to relatively small patches of the ocean to make a living.

Third, days-at-sea created an economic incentive for large vessels to shift their effort inshore. It makes sense: rather than wasting seven or eight hours steaming offshore, the captains chose to target coastal fish aggregations just minutes from the dock. Not surprisingly, the year after the system was implemented the government was forced to expand the inshore closures due to a dramatic increase in cod mortality.[11]

Fourth, for generations the inshore fleet conserved resources by harvesting several different fisheries seasonally, much as a farmer would rotate crops to preserve soil fertility. The practice increased in the late 1980s when NMFS asked fishermen to voluntarily conserve depleted groundfish stocks. But the days-at-sea allocation system was based on landings records from three "qualifying years" (1989, 1990, and 1991). Thus fishermen who shifted their effort to the shrimp or lobster fisheries in any one of those years, as instructed, were severely penalized.[12]

Finally, although inshore vessels make up nearly 80 percent of the fishery, and still only account for 20 percent of the total catch, they are spread out across hundreds of small ports from Montauk, New York, to Stonington, Maine.[13] Isolation and the numerous ecological, cultural, and political divisions have fragmented the fleet's collective bargaining power in the political process.

In the late 1990s, management decisions such as the Marine Mammal Protection Act and habitat closures accelerated the loss of small fishing businesses due to economic hardship. When NAMA was officially incorporated as a 501(c)3 based in Saco, Maine, in January 1997, the board of trustees and staff devised a work plan to immediately engage these disenfranchised communities in the political process by building a network of "community alliances" across the Gulf of Maine watershed. Over the next three years, NAMA helped form five such organizations: the Saco Bay Alliance in Saco, Maine; IFISH in Phippsburg, Maine; the Stonington Fisheries Alliance in Deer Isle, Maine; the New Hampshire Marine Coalition in Hampton, New Hampshire; and ProFish in Provincetown, Massachusetts.

However, NAMA quickly realized that regulatory changes were evolving so quickly they had to proactively engage the communities to be effective. "I think part of the problem had to do with the emotional impact of the rapid changes. Some of these people were just scraping by and didn't have the time or money to organize and go to one meeting after the other. In other words, the collapse of the fishery had impacted the ability of communities to emotionally engage in the decision-making process," said Pendleton.[14] He reluctantly resorted to single-interest lobbying tactics to fill in the gaps, speaking on behalf of inshore fishing communities at the council and in Washington. "To be honest, we had to fall back on some of the same 'business-as-usual' interest group advocacy that we had originally hoped to avoid, but it seemed like we were losing our fishermen by the day. We simply didn't have time to rebuild the whole system from scratch."[15]

COLLABORATIVE PROBLEM-SOLVING

The first industry-wide application of NAMA's organizational model came in 1998, after the government closed much of the inshore Gulf of Maine to protect dangerously depleted cod stocks (a consequence of the shift in effort caused by Amendment 5), which displaced hundreds of inshore operations from Massachusetts, Maine, and New Hampshire. To ameliorate the crisis, U.S. Senators John Kerry and Judd Gregg worked with their colleagues to provide a $5 million disaster relief package. But recognizing that the aid had the potential to ignite antagonisms between the fishery's different sectors, the politicians reached out for advice and NAMA was contracted to convene a series of meetings to determine how the money would be allocated. "It was clear that NMFS's preferred solution was to cut everyone a check and be done with it. But our conversations clearly showed that fishermen didn't want a handout,'" said Pendleton.[16]

Instead, the agreement developed an alternative solution reached by consensus, growing from an idea proposed by a group of New Hampshire fishermen. In return for the disaster aid, recipients would have to agree to "fish for data," that is, provide their expertise and equipment for use in marine research. (Alternatively, qualified applicants could fill out a socioeconomic survey supplied by NMFS.) Known as the "Tri-State Agreement," the plan outlined four principles concerning the disbursement of the relief package:

1.

All federal disaster relief funding should be expended to compensate fishermen

DISTRIBUTIION OF NORTHERN SHRIMP *(Pandalus borealis)*: ADULT FEMALES

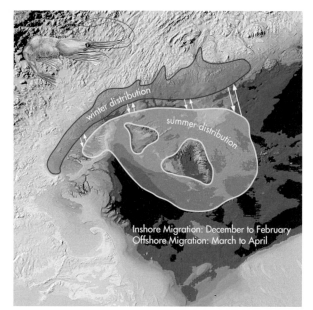

winter distribution

summer distribution

Inshore Migration: December to February
Offshore Migration: March to April

FIGURE 8:
After decades of depletion the Northern shrimp fishery (*Pandalus borealis*) is now one of the most robust in the Gulf of Maine. Collaborative research by fishermen and scientists has refined fishing gear so that shrimp can be captured with virtually no bycatch of regulated groundfish species.Unfortunately, competition by foreign farm-raised shrimp and a lack of processing plants have kept prices for the shrimp extremely low.

Graphic content developed by Adrian Jordaan, Curt Rice, Craig Pendleton, Sally Sherman, Steve Train, and Dan Schick. Shrimp from www.hafra.is. Concept by Heather Deese. Graphic by Ethan Nedeau.

for their lost fishing opportunities due to recent fisheries regulations in the Gulf of Maine cod fishery as soon as possible. A priority schedule should be created to compensate those fishermen who have lost all fishing opportunities first.

2.

In exchange for compensation for their lost fishing opportunities, fishermen will agree to participate in marine research programs created in partnership with the National Marine Fisheries Service (NMFS), the New England Fisheries Management Council, state agencies, universities and local fishing industry groups. The marine fisheries research would focus on cod tagging, effectiveness of closed areas, gear research and quantifying management measures involving the adjustment of fishing gear. Furthermore, the research plans would address the scientific needs of NMFS, the New England Fisheries Management Council and the fisheries entities of the states.

3.

No monies from the federal disaster relief funding should be used to administer the marine research programs. Rather the monies from the individual states, the Saltonstall-Kennedy grants program, Sea Grant, or private foundations should be used to administer any marine fisheries research program related to the federal disaster relief funding.

4.

It must be recognized that $5 million is not enough money to address
the economic hardship of the fishermen who derive their income from the
Gulf of Maine fisheries. Moreover, as New England Fisheries Management
Council reports foreshadow the imminent future fisheries closures to protect
species other than cod, additional funding must become available to assist
fishermen and shoreside infrastructure. The preservation of small community-
based fishing and related fishing industry corporations must be a priority to
ensure that a community-based fishing industry will be in existence when
fisheries rebound. Only a major investment in community-based fishing
industry corporations will ensure the future survival of family owned
businesses in light of current and future fishing regulations.[17]

The concept was institutionalized the next year with the creation of
the Northeast Consortium (NEC), a collaboration of four research institutions—
the University of Maine, Massachusetts Institute of Technology, Woods Hole
Oceanographic Institution, and University of New Hampshire's Institute for the
Study of Earth, Oceans, and Space—to encourage and fund research projects that
partner scientists and fishermen. In its charter, the consortium committed to
allocating 75 percent of all project budgets to industry partners and giving priority
to research topics generated by fishermen. Earlier versions of the model primarily
used commercial vessels as a cost-effective platforms, ignoring the important local
knowledge fishermen can offer the development of research questions in response
to emerging ecological changes.[18]

As landings continued to decline and regulations became tighter and
tighter over the next decade, the consortium not only became a valuable source of
information about the marine environment, but also an important source of ancillary
income for many vessels displaced by cuts in days-at-sea and closures. A good
example of this is the region's Northern shrimp (*Pandalus borealis*) fishery. Each
winter, the species migrates close to land to lay its eggs in the fertile inshore waters.
At the same time, groundfish leave the shallows for deeper environments offshore.
For generations, small vessels lacking the size and horsepower to safely roam the
Gulf of Maine to find groundfish in the winter were still able to make money on
shrimp. However, when cod, haddock, and flounder increasingly became scarce in
the late 1990s, the shrimp fishery's small mesh came under scrutiny for contributing
to mortality. By working with scientists like Dan Schick from the Maine

Department of Marine Resources, fishermen were able to prove that the environmental separation between finfish and crustaceans allowed shrimp to be caught without having an impact on struggling groundfish.[19]

Today, conservation gear innovations such as the Nordmore grate have been further refined through collaborative research partnerships and keep fishery some 97 percent free of regulated species bycatch. In 2007, stock assessments found one of the highest abundances of shrimp in nearly thirty years. The loss of fishing businesses and markets over the past fifteen years, however, severely impacted the industry's ability to cost-effectively harvest and sell shrimp. Fishermen fear that a similar fate could await them when iconic groundfish recover as scientists anticipate they will.

ACTING LOCALLY

While the Tri-State talks addressed the role fishermen can play in gathering ecological knowledge about the fishery and developing conservation gear technology, NAMA and its associates designed a plan to engage local communities in policy-making. Discussions with some eighty fishermen, physical and social scientists, and conservationists—drawing on many of the business insights raised during the early conversations with Dee Hock—culminated in "The Inshore Gulf of Maine Fisheries Conservation and Stewardship Plan." "The government's strong-arm approach of imposing blanket cuts didn't get at the basic problems of overfishing. The abundance, or scarcity, of fish and fishing behavior is the result of numerous factors. To be effective management needed to be more adaptable and more flexible," said Shelley.[20]

To get started, the group began to think of how regulations could address an ecosystem characterized by more diverse populations of groundfish than those recognized by the government's stock assessment protocol. The new concept of the marine system was based on generations of fishermen's observations and substantiated by research that Ted Ames, a fisherman and trained biochemist, was conducting at the time. Ames, who went on to win a McArthur "genius-grant" for his work, argues for the existence of local sub-stocks of groundfish and other species in the eastern sections of the Gulf of Maine.

For example, one of his papers convincingly shows that the region's fleet historically relied on one such coastal cod stock for much of the nineteenth century— fish that were severely depleted by highly mobile vessels from across the region in the 1980s and subsequently disappeared from stock assessments and landings reports. Ames believes that the persistently low numbers of groundfish in eastern Maine, even as populations have rebounded to the westward, is further evidence of the stock's distinctiveness. "Those fish won't come back until fishing rules recognize the presence of sub-stocks and create corridors that give fish the space to migrate back into the areas in substantial numbers," said Ames.[21]

To address these fine-scale attributes of the system, which almost all scientists who study the fishery now concede exist, the stewardship plan proposed adding an extra management boundary for Gulf of Maine, roughly along the 50-fathom curve from Cape Cod to the Canadian border. On the inshore side, fishermen would work with managers to create regulations in line with local ecological conditions. The plan assumed a new approach to fishing effort control by replacing blanket cuts with rules that specifically addressed how, when, and where the effort was directed.

For example, the plan proposed to eliminate night fishing, when fishermen believed species came out of hiding in droves to feed and reproduce. It also called for a reduction in the size of roller gear, which allows trawls to be towed over even the most rugged bottom. A limit on the number of gillnets that could be set was also proposed. Not only did the group believe the changes would promote conservation, but they thought it would be good for business by cutting overhead costs and time spent at sea.

To encourage long-term stewardship, it was proposed that fishermen commit to fishing in one area to make them more accountable for their fishing practices and subject to peer pressure from the other fishermen in the bioregion. Rather than distributing access to individuals based on catch history, the plan called for an allocation of fish to an area based on its particular maximum sustainable yield determined by NMFS trawl surveys and area-specific landings reports.[22]

Permit holders would then be granted fishing opportunities based on guidelines developed by expanded local advisory panels (similar to a format already used by the council to obtain information about local ecology and fishing practices). The panels would be required to include a diversity of interests and work with the government to monitor landings and adjust the pace of the harvest as recommended catches were approached. NAMA encouraged representatives of the offshore fleet to devise their own rules suitable for deepwater fishing, but they declined to participate.

Another crucial waypoint in the fishery's management came on May 1, 1998, when NMFS published new standards for overfishing set by the Sustainable Fisheries Act in the Federal Register. The law required regional councils to be in compliance with the guidelines by the following October. The New England council adjusted the fishery's optimum yields accordingly, at approximately twenty percent of each stock's total biomass, with Amendment 9 to the groundfish plan. But, bowing to pressure from powerful industry groups, the managers declined to implement regulations necessary to actually achieve landings in line with the new requirements. The council also failed to address the law's bycatch reduction standards. Notwithstanding, NMFS approved Amendment 9 on April 24, 2000.[23]

The following month, the Conservation Law Foundation, National Audubon Society, Natural Resources Defense Council, and Center for Marine Conservation (renamed the Ocean Conservancy) sued the agency again for failing to implement a management plan that met the imperatives of the Sustainable Fisheries Act. Six months later, Federal District Court Judge Gladys Kessler found for the plaintiffs on all counts and ordered the agency to immediately develop measures necessary to be in compliance.[24]

The industry's reaction to the decision reflected shifting attitudes of the fishery at the time, with numerous parties filing petitions to be included in the remediation. Four New England states; the cities of Portland, Maine, and New Bedford, Massachusetts, the Northeast Seafood Coalition, Associated Fisheries of Maine, Inc.; and the Trawlers Survival Fund joined the side of NMFS as defendant interveners. On the side of the conservationists, NAMA, the Cape Cod Commercial Hook Fishermen's Association (CCCHFA), the Stonington Fisheries Alliance, and the Saco Bay Alliance—predominantly inshore fishing interests groups—joined the conservationists as plaintiff interveners.[25] "I wasn't thrilled about collaborating with environmentalists," said Pendleton. "But it was becoming impossible to avoid the realization that if we didn't put the fish first, we were going to lose everything."[26]

Due to the complexity of the case, Judge Kessler urged the parties to find a more suitable compromise than she could formulate as a fisheries layperson. She also appointed an independent advisor to assist with her deliberations and made the court's mediation services available. In February 2002, both sides traveled to Washington, D.C., to participate in what the judge described as a "Herculean effort" to find consensus, but after a week-long stalemate, the talks reconvened in New England. The sticking point for the conservationists involved the use of total allowable catches (TAC). They argued that for nearly thirty years, managers permitted landings far in excess of the ocean's capacity to regenerate.[27]

At the urging of their fishing industry allies, though, CLF broke with the other conservation groups and opposed the use of a hard TAC. "We were convinced strict limits without a significantly upgraded data collection infrastructure and better observer coverage would lead to a derby fishery, dangerous conditions for fishermen, and negative conservation outcomes," said Shelley.[28] CLF, its industry partners, and NMFS eventually agreed to a set of temporary measures while the council worked on a long-term plan that complied with federal law. The other conservation plaintiffs, and the fishing groups that sided with NMFS, refused to sign the document.

One important facet of the case that has received little media or scholarly attention is the issue of "latent effort," a bureaucratic term that refers to fishermen who hold valid permits with relatively little catch history. "During the lawsuit some of the parties made a 'Boogey Man' out of latent effort. They minimized the problem down to simple math: Eliminate as many days-at-sea from the equation and it will minimize the pain to us," Pendleton said. "I remember saying to Peter Shelley and other environmentalists: 'How do you face yourself in the morning?' By buying into this crap you are penalizing the very people who are giving 100 percent conservation! But I wasn't able to totally convince them and it still bothers me today."[29]

The initial terms of the settlement agreement reached by NAMA, CLF, and NMFS proposed an allocation scheme based on the highest level of fishing activity over the previous three years. However, to ensure that the court order complied with the biological rebuilding provisions of the Magnuson Act, Kessler revised the qualification standard to the average effort over the same period, a seemingly small modification that would have eliminated as many as 350 inshore operations from the fishery. She later amended the order, explaining that her change would have interfered with the "complex and carefully crafted Settlement Agreement…would produce unintended consequences" and "cause grave economic and social hardship, as well as injustice to individuals families, [and] fishing com-munities."[30] Nevertheless, hundreds of smallholders still received only a modest allocation of days-at-sea.

By the time the rule changes mandated by the Settlement Agreement (known as Amendment 13) went to public hearings in 2003, stakeholder groups involved had well learned the game of fisheries politics. Leading up to the decision, industry and conservation groups brought on lawyers, policy consultants, and media specialists to attract support and attention to their agenda.

Once again, opposing policy proposals fell along the political and geographic lines. The Cape Cod Commercial Hook Fishermen's Association submitted a plan, which had social goals similar to those of the Gulf of Maine Stewardship strategy, to create a fishing sector. The plan imposed a strict total allowable catch based on NMFS data and a self-financed observer coverage program, but used the group's extensive landings of cod on Georges Bank to justify a 10 percent allocation of the resource to the fishermen. The sector's management boundaries were not based on actual ecological divisions and non-sector vessels could move in and out of the area. "We recognized area-based management as an important long-term goal for the fishery, but we just felt that it was not achievable politically. Our sector plan was a compromise between what we wanted and what we thought we could pass through the council," said Paul Parker, CCCHFA executive director.[31]

The Northeast Seafood Coalition submitted an alternative proposal for Amendment 13 that tried to give fishermen access to healthy stocks, without damaging species of concern, by dividing days-at-sea allocations into three categories: A-days for use on depleted stocks such as cod and yellowtail; B-days for recovered species such as pollock and Georges Bank haddock; C-days for fishermen who lost access under the settlement agreement; these days could only be used at a hypothetical point in the future when or if the fishery fully recovered.[32] "We tried to make light of the situation and called them 'C you later days,' because no one believed these people would ever fish again," Pendleton said.[33] The strategy garnered support from many in the fleet with vessels large enough to make the journey to Georges Bank, where haddock had rebounded significantly. For small boats from Maine such a lengthy voyage is simply out of the question.

NAMA submitted the Gulf of Maine stewardship plan. The area management strategy responded to the ecological and social realities of Maine's fishermen who had largely been cut out of the fishery due to the depletion of local groundfish stocks and the ensuing regulatory changes. During the hearings, the stewardship plan was criticized by opponents for trying to "re-allocate" fishing access standards codified by Amendment 5. Proponents of the approach countered that the days-at-sea system never reflected a fair allocation of fish and that their plan simply tried to return a balance to the distribution of fishing rights.

NMFS ultimately approved an amended version of the Northeast Seafood

Coalition proposal that cut days-at-sea by 40 percent across the board, but allowed fishermen who qualified for B-days to make up for the lost fishing opportunities. Over time, the B-Day program fell short of its intended goal, largely because it proved too difficult to harvest abundant species without also impacting the species of concern. The Hook Sector was also adopted. The Gulf of Maine stewardship plan was included as a "frameworkable item," ostensibly streamlining the full approval process for a later date.

In terms of future access, the most important policy development in Amendment 13 turned out to be an emergency days-at-sea leasing experiment proposed by NMFS in 2003. A press release at the time explained the rationale behind the move:

> The intent of the Program was to alleviate some of the negative economic and social impacts that may result from the reduced DAS allocations that will continue as a result of implementation of the final emergency rule. The Program was designed to maintain conservation neutrality, i.e., to maintain groundfish fishing effort close to the level that would be fished under the current management measures in the absence of the Program. The impetus for the Program was a request by the New England Fishery Management Council on May 20, 2002, that NMFS implement a DAS leasing program, on a permanent basis, through the most expedient mechanism.[34]

The program was generally opposed by inshore fishing groups, but received strong support from large operations and several active fishermen and absentee owners on the council. Between May 1, 2004, and April 30, 2005, more than 6,000 days were leased at a value of $2.5 million. The access tended to accumulate in the region's seafood capitals: operations from Portland leased 1,570 days (roughly 26 percent) of the fishery's total allowable days, New Bedford 1,060 (18 percent), and Gloucester 800 (13 percent). Subsequent analysis showed the program helped many operations turn a profit that year, but also led to a substantial increase in fishing mortality, upsetting environmentalists who were assured the plan would be conservation neutral. Furthermore, with days-at-sea held by fewer and fewer firms, catch history—the standard for allocation under quota management plans—continued to accumulate in the hands of fewer and fewer owners.[35]

Since Amendment 5, a few key private philanthropies had grown increasingly concerned about the direction of management in the country's most historic fishery and supported organizations, such as NAMA and Cape Cod Hook Fisherman's Association, to develop policy alternatives. In 2000, the Surdna Foundation (founded by John Emory Andrus in 1917) established the Andrus Family Fund to give Andrus family members between the ages of twenty-five and forty-five an opportunity to "develop meaningful opportunities for the entire Andrus family for public service, voluntarism, education, and training in philanthropy and non-profit work."[36]

Notably, the next generation of family members identified injustice and violence as areas they hoped to resolve with charitable giving and, more specifically, committed to support programs that addressed the psychological and emotional factors that sustain the problems. To that end, the group developed a philanthropic model based on William Bridges' theory of change (as articulated in *Transitions: Making Sense of Life's Changes*). The foundation model has been applied to police-community, identity-based, and conservation conflicts in urban settings as well as natural resource management disputes over public lands and water rights in the American West.

As the Amendment 13 debate unfolded in early 2003, Andrus invited NAMA and its Board of Trustees to participate in a conference that investigated the role social conflict played in the New England groundfish crisis. During the dialogue, Peter Shelley argued persuasively that many management failures had stemmed from a fundamental disconnect between the policy and the basic values of fishing communities. As a solution, he therefore proposed that the fishery's different interest groups collaborate on a shared vision of the future fleet in terms of vessel sizes, gear types, ports, and so forth, so managers could shape regulations that were in line with the fishery's social goals. The attendees believed such an exercise would be especially important as the government shifted toward market-based management strategies.

Andrus encouraged NAMA to develop the concept further in consultation with Dr. Jay Rothman, a Middle East scholar and founder of Aria Group, a conflict resolution firm that specializes in community reconciliation efforts built on dialogue and consensus. Rothman's approach to conflict resolution is grounded in contemporary humanistic scholarship and the collaborative change first described by Paulo

Freire's *Pedagogy of the Oppressed*, where communities become active agents in exploring the psycho-cultural roots of social problems. Participants then work together to find consensus on proposed solutions:

> ARIA-C3, formerly known as Action Evaluation, is a three-lens visioning process that helps individuals and groups collaboratively set and implement a value-driven agenda for change. Based in action research, conflict resolution and organizational learning theory, C3 combines research with action to guide change in complex environments. An effective and systematic social change and participatory planning process, C3 allows organizations and communities to accomplish their goals and corresponding action plans, while capturing citizen interest and commitment and building monitoring and evaluation into the infrastructure of the programming.[37]

Working with NAMA staff and an independent project advisor, Rothman and his staff customized a program known as the Fleet Visioning Project.

The process began with the distribution of more than 7,000 questionnaires to every groundfish permit holder in the fishery, as well as to researchers, business people, conservationists, and managers. Staff placed requests for participation in trade publications, made hundreds of phone calls, and visited commercial piers and fishing associations. Though numerous attempts were made to reach out to representatives of offshore interests, with one exception the group declined to participate.

The survey asked for basic demographic information—fishing gear type, percentage of income derived from commercial fishing, homeport, and so forth— but at the heart of the program were three interrelated questions:

1.
If anything were possible, what is your vision for the future of the groundfish fleet?

2.
Why is the future of the groundfish fleet important to you?

3.
How can your vision of the fleet be most effectively implemented, and what can you do to help?

By the end of the outreach phase, more than 250 stakeholders had responded by mail, email, and phone.

Organized by specialized computer software, the answers formed the foundation for ten meetings held near fishing communities across the Northeast (Long Island, New York; Narragansett, Rhode Island; New Bedford, Massachusetts; Bourne, Massachusetts; Manomet, Massachusetts; Gloucester, Massachusetts; Portsmouth New Hampshire; Portland, Maine; Rockland, Maine; and Winter Harbor, Maine). Not all respondents were able to attend the workshops, but the program was designed to incorporate every respondent's information into the dialogues. A final, region-wide meeting took place in Danvers, Massachusetts, in December 2005.

One of the most important outcomes of the project, and a principal focus of this chapter, are the responses to the "why" question in the survey. The answers came in the form of personal narratives, written and spoken. Such a storytelling exercise is particularly well suited for natural resource disputes because, as William Cronon noted in "A Place for Stories: Nature, History, and Narrative" (*Journal of American History*), people have a tendency to organize experiences in the natural world into stories that carry a moral lesson.[38]

Each meeting began with attendees telling their stories out loud as a way to connect participants emotionally to the problem-solving activity. According to Rothman, action evaluation supports a central principle of conflict resolution: an effectively designed process must engender ownership and participation by those most directly affected by the conflict.

Members of different stakeholder groups put forth strikingly similar values and goals, as illustrated in the following edited narratives (for the full text of these and other narratives, see Chapter 4):

> Over the years, I've seen everyone pointing a finger at everyone else, instead of dealing with the issues or trying to work them out together. There are so many different user groups; we've all got so many regulations against us that we are fighting amongst each other. We are pointing a finger at others to save ourselves. I would like to see more sharing and working together on issues of management conflicts, etc., so that we can stop pointing fingers at each other and start working cooperatively. Very rarely do we see different gear types at the same table. We have always cooperated with helping lobstermen take their gear out, and lobstermen have even sold us their permits. Though, normally, there is too much conflict for even this type of interaction. I wish I could say that I remember a time when there was more

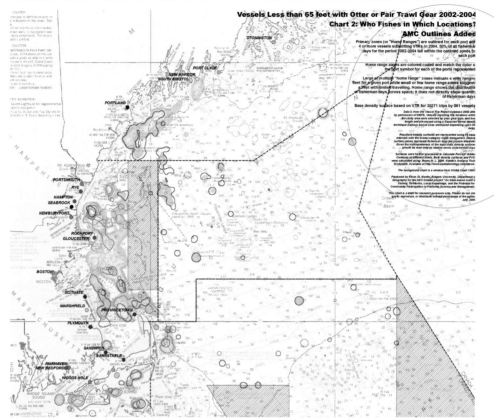

FIGURE 9:
Fishing patterns for vessels of less than 65 feet, based on Vessel Tracking Reports (VTRs) as compiled by Kevin St. Martin of Rutgers University. Colors indicate homeports. Note that the map shows only those grounds for which there are four or more vessels during 2004. The map stopped just east of Penobscot Bay because there weren't enough fishermen working in the northeastern Gulf of Maine to include. AMC outlines added.
Credit: Kevin St. Martin, Rutgers University

Primary zones (or "home ranges") are outlined for each port with 4 or more vessels submitting VTRs in 2004; 50 percent of all fisherman days for the period 2002-04 fall within the outlined zones for each port.

Home range zones are color-coded and match the color of the port symbol for each of the ports represented. Large or multiple "home range" zones indicate a wide-ranging fleet for a given port while small or few home range zones suggests a fleet with limited mobility. Home range shows the distribution of fisherman days across space; it does not directly show quantity of the days.

Base density surface is based on VTR for 30,271 trips by 361 vessels.

Data is from the Vessel Trip Report database 2002-04 by permission of NMFS. Vessels reporting trip locations within the study area were selected by year, gear types, and boat length and processed using a Gaussian kernal density technique (various kernal sites were used depending upon the data).

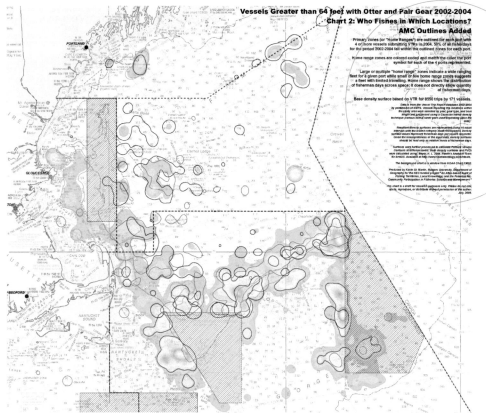

FIGURE 10:
Fishing patterns for vessels greater than 64 feet based on Vessel Track Reports (VTRs) as compiled by Kevin St. Martin of Rutgers University for the council. Colors indicate homeports. Note the map shows only those grounds for which there are four or more vessels during 2004. The map stops just east of Penobscot Bay because there were not enough fishermen working in the northeastern Gulf of Maine to include. AMC outlines added.
Credit: Kevin St. Martin, Rutgers University

Resultant density surfaces are represented by using sixteen equal intervals with the lowest category made transparent. Density surface values represent fisherman days per square kilometer. Given the incompleteness of the input data, density surfaces should be read only as relative levels of fisherman days.

Surfaces were further processed to calculate percent volume contours (PVC) at different levels. Both density surface and s and PVCs were calculated using Beyer H.L. 2004 Hawth's Analysis Tools for ArcGIS. Available at http://www.spatialecology.com/htools.

The background chart is a window from NOAA Chart 13003.

Produced by Kevin St. Martin, Rutgers University Department of Geography for the NEC-funded project "An Atlas-Based Audit of Fishing Territories, Local Knowledge, and the Potential for Community Participation in Fisheries Science and Management."

This chart is a draft for research purposes only and was used by permission of the author.

cooperation. I experienced cooperation once, when we were experimenting with aquaculture, and we worked hand-in-hand with scientists, government officials and other fishermen. I even did research on how aquaculture was done in other countries, to see how we could get our whole community together to work on it. I would like to see cooperation and less hostility between us because, when it comes down to it, we all want conservation. We need to work together to find solutions if we want the next generation to be able to fish.

Prior to working with fishermen, I worked with ranchers in south-west New Mexico where they were experiencing similar issues of loss of livelihood and a decline in their ecosystem. A decade ago ranchers were fighting a war of attrition. For every small victory there were many defeats. But rather than continue on this loosing course, they instead began to reach out to the traditional adversaries, to bring them together in finding where they had common ground. Through using science as a "community building tool," ranchers and researchers now have a collaboration that both improves the quality of the science, and provides credibility for all facets of the ranchers work. This is a message of hope because these communities once faced similar threats to fishermen, yet by working with a diversity of groups and turning adversaries into allies have turned things around. Ranchers who once saw no hope, now can see a future for their children and grandchildren in ranching. Fishermen have many of the challenges and opportunities. In addition to developing collaborative science the builds allies and credibility, a key point is to move beyond a focus on the ocean as a producer of commodities to consider overall ecosystem health. To move from a consumer, to a steward of natural resources and in doing so redefine the socioeconomic and ecological linkages between themselves and their environment.

I grew up in Waterville Maine, my dad was an insurance salesman who took me fishing and walking in the woods all the time. My dad was very business oriented but also had a strong conservation ethic. He taught me the importance of finding a balance between business and conservation. I remember when they used to send logs down the Kennebec River to transport them downstream. I would get upset when we couldn't go fishing during that time but my dad reminded me there were businesses that depended on sending the logs down the river. My dad also taught me the golden rule of putting back the small fish so that they would grow up and reproduce so that we would have fish for the future. These lessons stay with me today as I realize the need to find a balance between the needs of the fishing communities and the fish, between the in-shore and offshore areas. I feel like this is missing in today's fishery management system. To help achieve this balance today, I am working to help people recognize the ecological differences between in-shore and offshore areas, and the fisheries that work in them. I think that we need to have a system that provides incentives for larger boats to fish offshore, so that some fish are left inshore for the boats that don't have the option of going offshore. I don't see the balance between the health of fish populations and fishing communities in the management system right now. Although I have to say I feel a little more hopeful now than when I was a kid waiting for the logs go by. The Fleet Vision Project gives me hope because people are asking the important question of what we want the fleet to look like in the future.

Project staff analyzed all of the narratives and group discussion to identify common themes and values, then organized the information before giving it back to participants as a list of potentially shared goals and objectives. Participants accepted, rejected, or amended the list, thus maintaining ownership of the process.

The regimen was repeated at each workshop and the products served as a foundation for a final meeting, where representatives from the entire region worked to build consensus on a shared vision for the fleet. The vision embodied four principles that managers would consider when setting a new course:

1.

A geographically distributed commercial and recreational fleet that includes all gear types and boat sizes.

2.

An economically viable, safe, and sustainable fleet that works with shoreside infrastructure to supply seafood and job opportunities for coastal communities.

3.

Participatory, accountable, and decentralized governance structures at various scales that include local involvement in decision-making and maintain an adaptive regulatory environment.

Fishery stakeholders who exhibit stewardship of resources that is consistent with the long-term health and restoration of the marine ecosystem.

The products were published in a final report made available online and mailed to participants, council members, the NMFS regional administrator, and the NMFS executive.[39]

Some government officials and representatives of the offshore fleet, despite declining to participate, criticized the program for not representing the values of the whole industry. Lack of participation by key stakeholders is clearly an obstacle that must be addressed if the products of such an exercise are to prove sustainable for the entire fishery. Regardless, the program was effective in finding consensus among scientists, conservationists, and fishermen, all of whom recognized the negative ecological and social implications of the status quo. In the past, previous efforts by the same parties to influence policy was weakened when some groups and individuals pursued separate agendas. The division gave the relatively unified offshore sector more leverage to influence policies that furthered overfishing and consolidation.

INDUSTRY ALTERNATIVES IN AMENDMENT 16

Many of the stakeholders described above directly incorporated the common ground found in the Fleet Visioning Project in a policy proposal submitted for Amendment 16 to the groundfish plan. In 2006, after repeated failures of the days-at-sea program to bring about either ecological or social stability, the council called on the fishery to "think outside the box" and propose alternatives to the system. To that end, the Area Management Coalition—NAMA, CLF, the Nature Conservancy, Island Institute, Midcoast Fisherman's Association, Conservation Law Foundation, Downeast Initiative, the Ocean Conservancy, and Earthjustice—proposed a refined version of the Gulf of Maine stewardship plan. Following the lead of the Hook Sector, other groups submitted some nineteen similar proposals for different fishing interests across the region.

Like its predecessor, the area management strategy suggested drawing one additional management line roughly along the 50-fathom curve (or the 25600 and 25500 Loran lines) to separate the inshore and offshore ecosystems. This time, additional research indicating clear physical and biological distinctions between the bioregions and the fish that live there bolstered the initiative. Furthermore, the results of a study by Dr. Kevin St. Martin, a geographer at Rutgers University, supported the social justification for area management. His research, based on interviews with fishermen and thousands of vessel trip reports filed with NMFS, indicated a relationship between the region's fishing communities on land and the fishing grounds they use at sea.

St. Martin's report included color-coded GIS maps that linked a vessel's port of call with its reported fishing ground. "The maps clearly show differences in the fishing practices of the inshore and offshore fleets," said St. Martin. "What this means is that even under current regulations a form of spatially based management has emerged within the industry." The finding is important to supporters of area management because it undermines criticisms that claim the proposal is a kind of "sea-grab" designed to reallocate access. On the contrary, "the maps draw a kind of social landscape that give real contrast and definition to the meaning of existing fishing communities," he added.[40]

The plan proposed that fishermen declare a primary area for three years or longer, to ensure a commitment to stewardship that has been proven to arise the longer resource users reside in the same area. The strategy also outlined a governance system based on the existing structures used in groundfish advisory panels and the Cape Cod Hook Sector. Additionally, the plan's allocation scheme was not based on individual catch history, which has been severely distorted by localized groundfish depletions, Amendment 5, and days-at-sea leasing, but on the amount of fish NMFS scientists determined could be safely harvested from the area as indicated by stock assessment data and vessel trip reports. As with the Hook Sector, the community would voluntarily fish under a strict total allowable catch. All federally licensed fishermen, including C-day holders, would be allowed to declare a primary area as long as they followed the guidelines for fishing practices and the distribution of access established by the local community.

The Northeast Seafood Coalition also submitted a plan, known as the "Points System Management Program." The proposal suggested assigning a baseline number of points to all fishermen who received "A-days" in Amendment 13. The points are a kind of currency to be used to harvest fish, much as one would spend cash in a supermarket. However, to address the differential abundance of species the scheme assigned a "biological point value" (BPV) based on a species relative abundance: the more scarce, the higher the BPV (or by analogy, the cost of the product in the supermarket).

Operations would be allocated additional points according to a formula that included weighted considerations for vessel size, horsepower, and catch history. As fish were landed the points would be deducted from a fishermen's account managed by NMFS. A computer model would be used to increase a species' biological point value as it became increasingly scarce. Theoretically, a stock's maximum sustainable yield would never be reached because its BPV would approach infinity and therefore discourage its harvest before overfishing occurred.[41]

The point system was designed largely to address the industry's claims regarding fishing access. Because the system eliminated C-days, however, representatives of Maine's inshore fleet and other small holders objected to the formula. During hearings, the council and NMFS criticized the strategy for being too difficult to administer due to increased demands for landings data and monitoring. In fact, the managers laid the same accusation against the area management proposal, leading both groups to point out that for any management plan to be effective, including the status quo, a higher standard for monitoring and data collection would need to be implemented.

After a relatively short deliberation in late June 2007, the council rapidly advanced through a series of procedural maneuvers that tabled industry proposals until Amendment 17 was developed in favor of maintaining the days-at-sea system. (This uncharacteristic expedience led some observers to conclude that the managers had already agreed to the outcome without the benefit of public input.) The council also voted to further examine the sector proposals and initiated a debate about how access would be distributed.

The council's reliance on days-at-sea and catch history as the standard for future access in the fishery led critics to question whether financial conflicts of interest played a role, since most of the fishermen on the council invested heavily in days-at-sea leasing after Amendment 13. Proponents of alternatives argued that as current fishing interests assumed ownership of the fishing privileges in Amendment 16, whatever followed in Amendment 17—which would not be passed for at least three years—would be virtually irrelevant.[42]

In a related vote, managers approved a proposal by a council member to decrease the minimum length requirement from 19 to 17 inches for haddock captured on Georges Bank. The member said the change was necessary to avoid discards of undersize fish, which he publicly stated was at times in excess of 100,000 pounds a day.

Conservationists and small-scale fishermen in attendance criticized this proposal, which came as a surprise, as a reward for reckless fishing practices; they said it reversed hard-fought efforts to ensure that the region's juvenile groundfish were not harvested before they had an opportunity to spawn. Supporters of the move argued that the fishery was falling well short of the government's recommended harvest limit and that the fish were being lost to Canada's fleet, which was allowed to net the surplus landings under a controversial agreement between the two nations.

"The argument misses the point," said Paul Parker at the June meeting. "If you're getting into 100,000 pounds of bycatch, it's probably time to move to another fishing ground or adjust your gear. How long did it take us to learn the consequences of killing young fish? If you have a problem with the Canadian rule, bring it up with the State Department. They shouldn't be fishing on haddock before they've spawned either. This proposal is a step backwards."[43]

In early September 2007 the council's groundfish committee took up the question of how to allocate fish to the sectors. A number of council members argued for a scheme based only on catch history in preparation for the move to individual fishing quotas, which would give them ownership of the public resource. Chris Brown, a small vessel draggerman from Point Judith, Rhode Island, passionately argued for a variety of factors to be included in the allocation scheme: "Catch history only reflects the inshore fleet's lack of access due to regulatory changes and ecological factors out of their control. It is not fair to penalize fishermen for obeying the rules."[44]

Predominantly offshore interests argued that any boat that had not fished in the previous ten years should be eliminated entirely. The groundfish committee endorsed the proposal to eliminate inactive boats and also agreed to an allocation of white hake for one group's offshore sector that most scientists and fishermen believe is well in excess on the stock's optimum yield.

After the June vote, it had become increasingly clear that the sector concept—where a group of fishermen agree to work under a strict harvest limit and adopt a set of local rules to control the pace of fishing—would be the dominant management strategy for the next several years. In some ways the approach reflects a compromise between the competing policies pushed by fishermen, scientists, and conservationists for nearly fifteen years. For scientists and conservationists, it is a major step forward to have the fishery subject to a firm total allowable catch. For fishermen, sectors offer more flexibility to make business decisions and catch abundant species than the current days-at-sea management system allows.

But critics of sectors point out that the approach furthers ideas that have disadvantaged small-scale fishermen and rural fishing ports all along. First, the concept relies on arbitrary political boundaries instead of real ecological divisions, such as the one between the inshore and offshore Gulf of Maine. Second, the council's groundfish committee's endorsement of a sector allocation scheme based on catch history opened another phase of the longstanding debate over how access should be allocated. "First of all, I think we ought to be right upfront about what will happen with sectors without deciding as a community whether we will be managing in a different way," Robin Alden told *Commercial Fisheries News* in August 2007. "The fishery will be allocated. It will be done. We will be into IFQs. Before those decisions are made, we need to have serious discussions about how groundfish will be managed."[45]

To be sure, when this work went to press several fishing organizations had begun fundraising efforts to secure future access by "banking" federal multi-species permits for their members in anticipation of a shift to privatized management. Permit banking provides an opportunity for coastal communities to accumulate and hold access in perpetuity. The fishing rights can then be leased back to fishermen according to locally established guidelines and regional and national regulations. However, it is estimated that securing enough permits to keep even a small ground-fish port like Chatham, Massachusetts, profitable would take at least $10 to $15 million, a price simply out of reach for most of the remaining ports. Some national environmental groups like the Nature Conservancy have started to look at the concept as a way of ensuring long-term stewardship of the ocean, similar to how large swaths of land are held in trust with rules that regulate their use. However, recent history has shown that investing in New England's groundfishery carries more risk than the typical private philanthropy is comfortable taking on, and it is not clear how the approach would be nested in the current fishery management plan's rules and amendments.[46]

There are, in sum, a number of important value-laden questions that still need answers. We would do well to start with the ones originally laid out by the Fleet Visioning Project: If anything were possible, what is your vision for the future of the groundfish fleet? Why is the future of the groundfish fleet important to you? How can your vision of the fleet be most effectively implemented, and what can you do to help?

NOTES

1. Interview with author, March, 2007.

2. Ibid.

3. See Mitchell Waldrop's, "The Trillion-Dollar Vision of Dee Hock" in *Fast Company*, October 1996.

4. Interview with author, May 2007.

5. Interview with author, July 2007.

6. Interview with author, March 2007.

7. See www.namanet.org for the organization's mission, purpose, and principles.

8. See Giovanna DiChiro's "Nature as Community: The Convergence of Environment and Social Justice" in *Uncommon Ground*, 298–320, for an original discussion about the human impacts of ecological degradation.

9. Interview with Edward Ames, June 2006.

10. Fleming, 595–97.

11. Based on interviews with Pendleton, Shelley, Alden, Wells, and Rice.

12. Ibid.

13. The breakdown of percentage by vessel size comes from Tom Nies, senior staff at the New England Fishery Management Council. The discrepancy is likely greater today.

14. Interview with author, March 2007.

15. Interview with author, May 2006.

16. Ibid.

17. "Tri- State Agreement," U.S. Dept. of Commerce document, on file at Northwest Atlantic Marine Alliance.

18. See www.northeastconsortium.org for information about the development of its cooperative research program.

19. Interview with Dan Schick, February 2003. See *Collaboration*s that month at www.namanet.org

20. Interview with author, March 2007.

21. Interview with author, June 2006.

22. See the Inshore Gulf of Maine Conservation and Stewardship Plan at www.namanet.org

23. Fleming, 589-91.

24. Ibid., 591.

25. See footnote in Fleming on page 591.

26. Interview with author, June 2006.

27. Fleming, 594.

28. Interview with author, March 2007.

29. Interview with author, March 2007.

30. Fleming, 597.

31. Interview with author, June 2007.

32. See www.nefmc.org for a copy of the NESC Amendment 13 proposal.

33. Interview with author, May 2006.

34. NMFS Press Release May 27, 2003.

35. For technical analysis of the consolidation trends in the fishery see the New England Fishery Management Council Groundfish Plan Development Team's December 29, 2005 report:
http://nefmc.org/nemulti/frame/fw42/appendix_I.pdf. Also see
http://www.nmfs.noaa.gov/msa2007/Framework42Reportto
CongressFinalFinal.
pdf.

36. See www.affund.org for an overview of the foundation's mission.

37. See www.ariagroup.com for information about the organization's humanistic approach to conflict management.

38. See William Cronon's "A Place for Stories: Nature, History, and Narrative," *Journal of American History,* 78: 4, for an excellent review of the role of storytelling in the historical craft.

39. The complete Fleet Visioning Project report and more narratives are available by contacting www.namanet.org.

40. "Fisheries for the Future" symposium lecture at the Island Institute, August 13, 2007.

41. See www.nefmc.org for a copy of the Points System plan.

42. See www.nefmc.org for a copy of the Amendment 16 final rule.

43. Interview with author, June 2007.

44. Interview with author, June 2007.

45. Plante, Janice. *Commercial Fisheries News.* august 2007.

46. Interview with Paul Parker, September 2007.

CHAPTER 4

PORTRAITS AND NARRATIVES

PHOTOGRAPHS BY REBECCA HALE

DAVID GOETHEL

Owner/Captain

F/V *Ellen Diane*

Hampton, New Hampshire

I have done this all my life. I started when I was thirteen, recreational when I was seven. I like to catch stuff and I don't like to sit around. And I like to be my own boss. What made America great was entrepreneurship. We can't have an unlimited number of entrepreneurs in the fishery anymore. It use to be if you were a highline fisherman, you brought home a lot of fish. Highlining now is more complex; it includes management solutions, reducing bycatch, catching the right kind of fish at the right time. We've been trying to cut down on the mortality, but we need to get out of our box.

New England is the only region that has strong fishing communities left. We have a strong tie to the ocean here and I want to see those ties preserved. My family is my community. I have a house, garage, two kids through college, all paid for through fishing. If we disappeared tomorrow, my town wouldn't know and wouldn't care. When they see us, we're working on the dock in the daytime because we can't go fishing.

The way I was brought up is that you're supposed to leave the place better than when you came. Way back when I was in my teens, I was going to fishery meetings. There has always been a disconnect between science and management, and it was a battle mentality. We marched on the Massachusetts State House en masse and confronted the federal and state legal authorities and they backed down. We decided that was effective fisheries management: march up to the state house with a harpoon, threatening to beat to a pulp anyone who disagreed, and stay until you get your own way. I think we've always danced around the issue that we have a finite resource and an infinite number of people who want access to it.

GEOFFREY SMITH

Marine Program Director

The Nature Conservancy

Portland, Maine

I grew up in Waterville Maine. My dad was an insurance salesman who took me fishing and walking in the woods all the time. My dad was very business oriented but also had a strong conservation ethic. He taught me the importance of finding a balance between business and conservation. I remember when they used to send logs down the Kennebec River to transport them downstream. I would get upset when we couldn't go fishing during that time, but my dad reminded me there were businesses that depended on sending the logs down the river. My dad also taught me the golden rule of putting back the small fish so that they would grow up and reproduce so that we would have fish for the future.

These lessons stay with me today as I realize the need to find a balance between the needs of the fishing communities and the fish, between the inshore and offshore areas. I feel like this is missing in today's fishery management system. To help achieve this balance today, I am working to help people recognize the ecological differences between inshore and offshore areas, and the fisheries that work in them. I think that we need to have a system that provides incentives for larger boats to fish offshore, so that some fish are left inshore for the boats that don't have the option of going offshore. I don't see the balance between the health of fish populations and fishing communities in the management system right now. But I have to say I feel a little more hopeful now than when I was a kid waiting for the logs go by. The Fleet Vision Project gives me hope because people are asking the important question about what we want the fleet to look like in the future.

RENIER NIEUWKERK

Owner/Captain

F/V *Hannah-Jo*

Kennebunk, Maine

I loved fishing since I was a kid. I grew up in a fishing community. I used to see gillnetters come in the harbor deck loaded with fish. They would cut and gut next to the pier and I thought, "I want to do that." I was also attracted to fishing because of the lifestyle. I liked the lobstermen and fishermen. They seemed to have their own micro-community. They worked independently but they would work together when they had to, like when there were storms and traps were snarled up. I have always wanted to fish commercially, and I worked hard to be able to. I still like fishing because I enjoy finding the fish. I like trying different gear types, and I like trying to catch different species. It is never the same for me; there is always more to learn, that is what keeps me interested. I would like to see the fishing industry go in a sustainable direction.

NORMAN C. EDWARDS, JR.

Owner/Captain

F/V *Petrel*

Amagansett, New York

We are at a low point right now. That decline started in the late 1980s. For the inshore fishery the winter flounder stock started to drop because of water quality. When the brown tide came, the spawning fish started their decline. The government based days-at-sea on landings from 1996 to 2001, when they were at an all-time low. During the same period, the striped bass were coming up at record highs.

What is needed in managing fisheries is trying to set the balance in managing different species. We aren't there yet, but we need to start recognizing the need for that. The conditions of the inshore fishery weren't taken into account when the criteria for days-at-sea was developed.

I am at zero days-at-sea. That has me upset, because it makes my permit almost useless. When I look at the blackback flounder and the income potential of that when the stock returns, I could make a living on that in March, April, and May. I think that income is important and a healthy inshore winter flounder stock would extend my fishing season. I think that potential income is important and I want to emphasize that.

Right now I'm fishing approximately 150 days a year on mid-Atlantic stocks on a 40-foot boat. I started fishing when I was six years old. I'm a twelfth generation in my community, and my family's been in the fishing business since the late 1600s. Heritage is very important to me. My father died at sea the year before I was to return home to fish with him. It's important to me to preserve that heritage that has gone on for generations. I first had a passion for fishing when I was seventeen and I came home from the Coast Guard and my dad had an extra trawler that he let me use to fish for yellowtail flounder for three weeks. I took classmates from my academy class and they got tired after three days. But for me, there was nothing like the independence out there, for I felt that I was doing my thing and making a living in an environment that I love. Whenever they have the opportunity, my children and grandchildren are out there fishing with me, just as I did with my father and grandfather. We went groundfishing, purse seining, and swordfishing every summer when I was growing up. That's the experience that I want to share with my children and my grandchildren.

MIKE CROCKER

CHRIS BROWN

Owner/Captain

F/V *Grandeville Davis*

Point Judith, Rhode Island

I was raised by my grandfather and from this I walked away with a good sense of right versus wrong. When I got my first boat, I participated in the largest stock decline in history. I really don't feel good about this. If the fishery is healthy, sound, and vibrant, the family nature will be preserved in New England. We have to individually look at how we have gone wrong and address these issues. Conservation starts with the guy in the mirror. We can't expect that someone else is watching out for our livelihood. Commercial fishing, thirty years ago, was much less a rush to get rich, it was about the rush to have a good lifestyle. Healthy stocks are tied to a healthy lifestyle. This is one of my attempts to right the ship. I don't want to work eight days a week, twenty-six hours a day to make ends meet. Responsibility happens with a lot of little acts. We have to treat the fishery like we own it, not like something we take advantage of. This conservation is an ongoing mindset.

HEATHER DEESE

Marine Science and Policy Consultant

Union, Maine

I feel deeply connected to the ocean and I feel responsible to do what I can to ensure its health, including clean water and thriving marine life. We all share responsibility for taking care of the earth—land and water. I grew up spending a lot of time on the water and have always felt a deep connection to the ocean. I'm dedicating my career to gaining knowledge of it. But where I lived in suburban Boston and how I spent time on the water, I never knew people who worked on the water. Closest I came was watching fishing boats sway past us on our sailboat, rigs hauled up and heading home through Vineyard Sound.

In the past few years I have met and worked with lots of people who live and work on the water in New England. They have my respect and admiration. These guys risk their lives to go out into the ocean to harvest the fish to make a living. I go out to do research in government funded boats that are safe.

I also respect the rest of the ocean, the fish, plankton, and the system itself. We have done a pitiful job taking care of the ocean. I'm very saddened by this poor job and the greed that exists. This motivates me to help figure out how we can do a better job. I'm driven by the respect and the sadness. Our history of the use of this earth—land and ocean—is one of people not doing a good job of respecting the ecological systems in which they work, taking more than is healthy. Very few people work off the ocean any more; we have not left much.

DAN DUNBAR

Captain/Owner

F/V *Little Mako*

Swampscott, Massachusetts

I've done two things: I've played hockey and I've gone fishing. My dad is an electrical engineer. I'd have to go way back to find a historical connection to fishing. Lobstering won't fund my lifestyle. When I was a kid I loved it because everyone was having fun hanging around and learning so many different things. working on engines, hauling boats out. It was a lot of fun working on that stuff and hearing the stories. I could've played hockey, but I was 100 percent fisherman. It was a waste of time for me to go on to higher education, but I could go out and run a boat as an eighteen-year-old and be as successful as anyone else. Trying to find something else with that kind of individuality is a tough thing to do. When they stick you with these problems, the solutions aren't easy. I like to go out on the water; I enjoy the monkfish, and I have a huge smile on my face when I see a cod coming onto my boat. There have been so many changes in the past seven years. I have a long way to go because I'm still young and have a family to support and kids to send to college. How many things do you really know in life that you can go out and make a good living doing? How many people look back on their life and think about what could have been? My thing is POWER. It makes me who I am today. It's about controlling my own destiny. There are other things I could do, but what I want to do is get on my boat and go fishing like I have since I was about five years old.

CHARLES CURTIN

Biologist

Massachusetts Institute of Technology

Cambridge, Massachusetts

Prior to working with fishermen, I worked with ranchers in southwest New Mexico where they were experiencing similar issues of loss of livelihood and a decline in their ecosystem. A decade ago ranchers were fighting a war of attrition. For every small victory there were many defeats. But rather then continue on this losing course, they instead began to reach out to the traditional adversaries, to bring them together in finding where they had common ground. Though using science as a "community building tool" ranchers and researchers now have a collaboration that both improves the quality of the science, and provides credibility for all facets of the ranchers' work.

This is a message of hope because these communities once faced similar threats to fishermen, yet by working with a diversity of groups and turning adversaries into allies have turned things around. Ranchers who once saw no hope, now can see a future for their children and grandchildren in ranching. Fishermen have many of the same challenges and opportunities. In addition to developing collaborative science that builds allies and credibility, a key point is to move beyond a focus on the ocean as a producer of commodities to consider overall ecosystem health. To move from a consumer, to a steward of natural resources, and in doing so redefine the socioeconomic and ecological linkages between themselves and their environment.

JOHN MESCHINO

Owner/Captain

F/V *Triple J-BE*

Hull, Massachusetts

I hate to see anything killed needlessly. In the fishing industry, if there is one big problem in my opinion, it's the things getting killed needlessly. I own a lobster boat, and when I see small fish on my deck people laugh at me when I flip them back in the water. For example, the typical cod fishermen will throw the small fish back so that these don't count toward reaching the legal limit. The chance of survival for these little fish is nill. Although I have to throw it back because of the limit. I find this incredibly wasteful. When the dragger pulls the net up, whatever he pulls up he should keep, utilizing everything he catches, and not throwing away the "bycatch." In lobstering, it is different, because the lobster is going to survive if I throw it back in. This is difficult for draggers to do, because a lot of things get stuck in the nets. I knew a guy who had to throw back 1,500 lbs of soft-shell lobsters because of restrictions, and all of them got crushed during reentry.

Conservation is important to me, meaning we need to utilize everything we pull over the side. Once you are in the industry and go through the various stages, you begin to see waste that goes over the side. You see firsthand all the fish you throw over float back up, dead. The value I have for conservation is in conflict with the regulations that we have to abide by. Regulations are put into place to give uniformity, that's why we have size limits and timing of reproduction—it is all a life process. We need to abide by the natural regulations of the sea and not waste any of the precious resources that come onto our decks.

KEN LA VALLEY

Fisheries Scientist

University of New Hampshire Cooperative Extension/New Hampshire Sea Grant

Durham, New Hampshire

I would hate to see the small town atmosphere of New England disappear. With the further reduction in days-at-sea we are seeing a fleet consolidation and a loss of a cultural heritage. I would hate to see the northeast fishing industry become industrialized, and with it the loss of our coastal New England small town charm. I want to support the small vessel owner-operator and whatever changes to the regulatory framework that need to occur to maintain that fleet structure. I believe there will always be a commercial fishing community in New England, but will it be run by a corporation, community, or individuals? I'm not sure.

I grew up in a very small town in New Hampshire, in a family that loved to hunt, fish, and enjoy the outdoors. It was a family connection—we have our own hunting and fishing areas that have been used for generations. I remember going fishing with my father, brother, older sister, cousins, and uncles. It was the thing to do and it strengthened our bond. You looked forward to doing it. The same is even more true for coastal families that have generations of commercial fishing history. We need to make it possible to keep that culture alive for the people who grew up there, and for their families.

MIMI BECKER

Economist

University of New Hampshire

Durham, New Hampshire

My father was a commercial fisherman on Lake Superior and he helped collapse that fishery. He regretted it the rest of his life as he had to go find a new profession.

The Great Lakes fishery has been collapsed until relatively recently, and even now you can't safely eat the fish from most areas in the Great Lakes. There are very small commercial fisheries on Lakes Superior, Huron, and Erie, and none on Michigan and Ontario.

Since I've been on the East Coast and in New England, I've seen not just the decline of fish populations, but the decline of communities and cultures. I remember sitting down to breakfast after the judge made a difficult fisheries management decision, to see a room full of grown men in tears because of what the implications were. We need to enable people to continue to survive economically and culturally in communities that have a healthy and sustainable fishery. To me an ecosystem is a system that includes the entire food web, including fishermen and rest of us as well as our communities and their cultural and institutional systems.

DANA MORSE

Extension Associate

University of Maine Cooperative Extension/Maine Sea Grant College Program

Walpole, Maine

A diversified fleet is key to sustaining not just groundfish but all fisheries. The lobster fishery is especially vulnerable to change or decline. This is not just about groundfish, but about sustaining all small and multi-use fisheries on the coast of Maine. From the point of view of a resource user, I began to work in the marine world in 1991.

Sustainability goes beyond the resource to the people dependent on it. For example, I grew up in New Hampshire, where we used to hook and line blackbacks. I fish recreationally, I hunt, I used to cut wood in high school; I'm a resource user. So, when I say sustainability, I include resource use, but also making sure they are available for future generations. When I drive down the road, with the farmers cutting hay, I think about the longevity of the fields that have been used for so long now, and wonder if they stand up to development pressure. When I go on a boat, I see the fish coming up in the net and wonder the same thing. So, I do think about sustainability, but am hopeful because of the creative and energetic people with whom I work.

BILL STONE

Retired Professor, University of Maine

F/V *Puff*

Prospect Harbor, Maine

I grew up in two small towns in Maine. My mother was from Camden, where I was born. When I was in the third grade, we moved to Edgecomb, where my father took over the country store and post office from his mother, who had been the postmaster for fifty years. Many different types of people shopped in the store and I knew them all. I remember being inducted into the grange when I was twelve years old, so I had a real sense of what a community should be. In high school we moved back to Camden, and during those years, I got to understand the Downeast coast working on the vacation schooners during the summer. After going to college, I left Maine only to come back for a career at the University of Maine.

After retiring I came back to the coast at Prospect Harbor where I got involved with the community and did some lobster fishing. I watched the shift in lifestyles along the coast, with the prices of real estate going up and the properties being bought up by seasonal folks. This trend concerned me so I began to work with the Downeast Groundfish Initiative. I value the coastal way of life and the fishing communities that exist here.

ELMER BEAL

Anthropologist

College of the Atlantic

Bar Harbor, Maine

I fear that a torrent of words would not be enough to change this world. I grew up in a small town and my family were fishermen. The fishermen lived next to the water in nice homes. There were forty to fifty fishermen in our community who were good, prosperous folks. These people were thrifty, buying boats with cash, saving what they made, and giving back to their communities. Our country is losing this hardworking ethic; the big interests are ruining the industry. In this area, there were hundreds of fisherman, now there are none in this room because they are gone or they are so heartbroken that they couldn't show up here today. Everyone loses something when this way of life is gone.

ROBIN ALDEN

Executive Director

Penobscot East Resource Center

Stonington, Maine

My father was a schoolteacher who took jobs working on the water in the summer so I grew up helping him. Later, when I moved to Maine, I became aware, writing for a local newspaper, that the whole town ran on fishing, yet it was invisible to the shore-side world.

By talking to fishermen, I also became aware of how much they know about the resources that they chase—knowledge gained through an intuitive process. Sitting in a conference, I heard a fisherman talking about shrimp. He clearly knew an incredible amount about shrimp. There was a scientist there who clearly knew a lot about shrimp as well. They were at odds, not able to hear each other. The fisherman, pointed down to his own shirt and said, "I have paint on my t-shirt; I bet you've never had paint on your t-shirt!" This gave me the idea to start a newspaper where the knowledge that each one had could be shared in a non-threatening way over and over again each month so that hopefully both worlds could learn to talk with each other.

My naturalist father taught me to care about the environment. When I found fishing, it seemed perfect: you could make a living forever by taking care of the resource. Fisheries policy drives us toward alienation and greed; yet there is the seed of the answer in our traditional communities in those with a connection to the resource. This connection between people and a diversified fishery is the seed of how we might be able to live on this planet with balance.

TED AMES

Lobsterman and Biochemist

Stonington, Maine

I used to groundfish in various ways, but times have changed. Back then I used to average about half a million pounds per year, for up to five months of fishing. A few years earlier, my brother's best day handlining was 18,000 pounds. Before that, my dad used to be in the million-pound-a-month club when he skippered one of the fleet of sixteen draggers based in Rockland. You don't find anybody catching fish like that anymore because the fish are gone.

The technology we had back then allowed us to wipe out fisheries, long before the sophisticated technology of today came along, and we almost succeeded. What we see today is not something that just jumped out of a box.... It's been a long time coming to where stocks are today. The hope is that we can learn to constrain our technology so that we can slow harvesting to a rate the stocks can stand. We need to protect the remaining fish from being over-fished, so we can rebuild the stocks.

CAPTAIN JAY MICHAUD

Owner/Captain

F/V *International Harvester*

Marblehead, Massachusetts

The reason I got into fishing goes back a long way, and marrying a fisherman's daughter sure helped. When I was a little boy I discovered that my neighbor was heading out to his boat at 4:30 and at 4:15, I would be in his truck waiting with my sandwich to go with him.

What I do for a living is quite noble in my mind. I heard someone talking about loving fish. What I do and what my wife does…we put the freshest, all-natural, no preservatives, nutritious food on the table of America and the world. We bring in the best. We bring lobster in; we sell lobster live. It's the only animal that you can buy today that's still alive, and there's nothing fresher than that. We provide this to people looking for a good source of nutrition. It makes me very proud to know that I'm a part of that. It makes me feel very good to know that I'm a farmer. Until crustaceans get to a certain size, they go in and out of traps that act as feeding stations on the bottom of the ocean. When the feed is there the animals are there, and when the feed is gone the animals are gone. That's what my job is and that's as noble a calling as you can get.

I'm also in the happiness business. There isn't a soul in the world who gets lobster because they're hungry. They have a lobster dinner because they are celebrating something: a wedding, a birthday. My son and I both have state gillnet permits. We fish under a strange checkerboard of rules and regulations of the day. It's important to everyone that there be a viable fishing community and a strong fishing fleet. Gloucester is falling apart, but without Gloucester for supplies and infrastructure, the other communities won't be able to survive because there is such interdependence. We need our fishing communities—with Gloucester as a hub—to be very strong.

SUSAN S. MICHAUD

Owner/Captain

F/V *A Touch of Gray*

Marblehead, Massachusetts

My father was a free-spirited fisherman. Everyone in the family was involved in the business. Then, as he started to fish, things started to change and trawls came into existence.

Talking about family, most dads have sons to come in to take over the business. My father had three girls, so I ended up being his "son." He taught me to go lobstering. He put me in contests with all males to go fishing. I won a fishing contest in Boston and the *Globe* had to change my name because I was supposed to be a boy. In high school I fished fifty traps. I made enough money to buy a car, one of the few in my community. I went out of the industry for a while, then went back into it when my husband wanted to run a co-op with my son, who now runs the boat. So, it's three generations in the business now. The best times we ever had were spent together on the boat.

FRANK MIRARCHI

Owner/Captain

F/V *Barbara L. Peters*

Scituate, Massachusetts

I've fished for the last forty-two years. I've been on the water since I was ten, when my parents moved to a coastal town. In high school, my friends and I were fishing groupies, hanging around the fishing docks, wanting to be future fishermen. Out of high school, I didn't want to go to college; I wanted to be a fishermen. My dad made a deal with me, that if I would graduate from college, he would support me to become a fisherman. So after college, my friends from high school became my crew, but more than that, we were friends fishing together. I was pretty successful, adapting to the technologies of the industries, all the while continuing the relationship of friendship with my crew members. We shared work, risks, and rewards. The work has been less difficult this way; everyone is fulfilling a role, and as a team we've been successful together. My business has paid for a lot of houses and college educations.

I've helped people through fishing. Fishing is not about killing fish; it is about feeding people. We see the product as beneficial to our communities. Many years ago, our town used to have a cultural celebration and one year, I was in charge of the fish dinner, so we caught two or three hundred fish. I filleted it all myself in one day. A friend of mine, a restaurant owner, cooked the fish, throwing in the side dishes. We fed three hundred people; everyone loved it and complimented the fish. This felt really good.

I've devoted my life to it and it's too late to do anything else. My younger son wanted to be a fisherman, and I had some angst over it because I wasn't sure if it was going to be a good move or not. We've been successful in rebuilding stocks, but we're lacking in building a future for fishermen. My son's and his friends' futures are not yet stable.

I love fishermen. I really enjoy hanging out with fishermen and fishing communities. I always want to go hang with the fishermen on the pier and that's what I really love to do. I don't want to see that culture disappear and I'm really afraid that it might. We could easily disappear, just like the cowboys in the West. It's interesting that as soon as land reverted into private hands the cowboys disappeared; I don't want to see that happen to fishing. But I can see that happening because of the enormous wealth that can be made from the East's fish stocks. It would really bother me to see someone who has nothing to do with the fishing culture of today end up with the fishing stocks tomorrow.

106 SHARING THE OCEAN

HOWDY HOUGHTON

Retired Fisherman

Bar Harbor, Maine

I feel very close to our local society and I always wanted to bring what I catch to the local community instead of shipping it. Seafood—caught, processed, and distributed locally—broadens community support for local producers, reduces cost to local consumers, decreases distribution time and effort, keeps more in the local economy, and most importantly, connects the local community with the fishermen and the ocean.

I identify strongly with the local food system on Mount Desert Island, after marketing my catch here for many years. In the 1990s I hand picked and delivered mussels to twenty local restaurants and had personal relationships with all those folks, some developed in the 1970s, selling them scallops, and in the 1980s, groundfish through a local fish market. These personal connections were as important to me as the financial gain, knowing the locals appreciated the freshest seafood and respect for the hard work it takes to produce it.

Through the 1980s, the Bar Harbor groundfish fleet grew to about fifteen small, seasonal and medium-to-large full-time draggers that landed a lot of fish. We did our share of reducing the fish stocks, as did several other eastern Maine ports. Presently groundfish landings are almost nonexistent in eastern Maine, so fish, fresh off the boat, is rare.

I've spent much of my life harvesting seafood and am proud to have provided fresh local seafood to my community. In the future, if groundfish stocks rebound in eastern Maine coastal waters, we need to consider just how dependent our communities are on fisheries as a food source and take care of the fish. We must use wise local stewardship to maintain healthy local seafood ecosystems for future generations, and for cultural, economic, and local seafood security.

CRAIG A. PENDLETON

Owner/Captain

F/V *Ocean Spray*

President/Owner, PENDLE, Inc.

Saco, Maine

I'm concerned about the way we're making decisions and that we're making decisions without any forethought and goals. I'm concerned that my son doesn't want to go fishing and that interrupts the fishing heritage that my family has had for a long, long time.

I've been trying to find ways of getting more people involved. I lie awake at night trying to figure out what to do. As long as I stay concerned, it keeps my mind looking toward the future and trying to figure out what we can do to make this work better. I want future generations to see what it's like to go out and fill the boat and make money.

Hope is a commodity that I would compare to the oil situation right now. For a lot of us it's running dry. Every time there's a glimmer on the horizon, something happens and it strips that hope away. I consistently try to keep my battery charged with hope that things are going to get better.

I love owning my boat and having a connection to fishing. I've been fishing since I was nine. At age twelve I made more than my mother. I would love to get fishing back to that point and make it fun again. I constantly wonder who's going to be standing over the pier smiling and proud that I brought in food? The public needs to realize that there are people and organizations working very hard to make fishing more sustainable. The hope I get out of work like this is that eventually this new way of organizing and decision-making will become the norm—all the different people come together and make decent decisions before they impact five or six hundred people who never had the chance to see the paper or comment on what was going to happen to them.

A lot of good opportunities came later in my life. I went to the University of Rhode Island commercial fishing and marine technology program. It was a really important personal decision and it set the stage for my future while giving me practical experience. Looking back, what makes me the most proud is that when I was nine years old, my mother let me go out on the boat because she saw the passion that I had and she knew there were good men to work with down at the pier. Her ability to see the positives, above a mother's normal concerns for a child, was extraordinary.

TIMOTHY FEEHAN

Safety, Quality, and Environmental Engineering Sector

Perot Systems

Pembroke, Masachusetts

I grew up visiting Point Judith and I remember the port being full of fishing boats with bustling fish houses and infrastructure. I've seen it shrink and change, and as that infrastructure is lost you lose the people and the livelihood. I see it as a livelihood and a way of life that has always been here and is a part of the history of New England. There's also the ability of people being able to make a living and feed themselves and pass this tradition down to their kids that seems to be lost.

My family wasn't associated with fishing, but I felt connected because we were down there so often. Perhaps my love of being on boats and watching fishermen on the boats is what led me to do what I do today. The experiences as a kid of being down there and seeing the boats come back in made me want to be a part of it. I wanted to see what it was that fishermen did when they went out to sea. I didn't have that opportunity until I went out to sea myself to observe what the draggers, lobster boats, longliners, gillnetters, and fish weirs did. I miss the trips and being out there on the boats and working with their crews.

CURT RICE

Captain

F/V *Robert Michael*

Portland, Maine

I was raised thirty-five miles south of Boston. It's hard for people in this room to imagine now, but it was rural then. I lived on a river. I used to lie in the woods and listen to the crows and have deer walk up within ten feet of me while I lay in the meadow. Living. Didn't even want to go to work. Waste of time going to work... miss too much. Took me twenty-eight years to figure out how to go fishing, and that was the best move I ever made. Have an agricultural background...processed food, dairy, plants, food. Church background—I was in every youth group, student council—a thousand miles an hour for a kid. All I wanted was to live. Slow, comfortable pace. Went fishing, tripled my shoreside income as a deckhand. A hundred and forty days on the ocean, 187 days out of 365—you know how much free time that gives you to lie in a meadow? Very selfish? Very self-centered? I don't apologize for that. It's what I do. It's what I want to do.

I come to these meetings because they want me out. I worked for the Department of Agriculture right out of college in Boston, Massachusetts. I was on the job four months and I said, "Boss, what are we doing, we're taking the markets away—what are we doing?" He said no no no—and explained how that wasn't what we were doing. It didn't make sense to me. But in one year I knew that my government wanted the dairy business consolidated. That's when I first started fishing and kept fishing for thirty years. I retired from fishing about seven years ago. I have an analytical tech background and for two years I couldn't get a job in Portland, where we have several labs doing research on pet products. I thought I'd find a job in their labs, but I couldn't even get my foot in the door. We have food companies, too, but thirty years ago I worked for a company where they didn't want the union in the house and that industry has a long memory. After a couple years off the water, I got back to it on a research vessel.

We know a dairyman who is still in the business. I want to hang in and survive as a fisherman, like he has as a dairyman. I want to be like him. He hung in there survived as a farmer. I want to make it as a fisherman. The more I produce, the more I earn; the more competent I am, the better I do. How do we make this business self-supporting? That's why I'm here this afternoon.

JENNIFER BREWER

Geographer

New Harbor, Maine

I have been a part-time or full-time resident of Maine and New England coastal communities all my life. I spent many years working in shoreside restaurants and other businesses. I have lived in two fishing-dependent households. I have lived and worked around the fishing industry, but I do not rely directly on fishing for my personal income. I now do research and policy work.

Fishermen notice how our environment is affected by changes in climate, weather, water and air quality, shorelines, etc. Like farmers, their livelihoods depend on careful daily observations. When young people learn to fish from family and community members, they acquire precious skills, and ecological and cultural knowledge that would otherwise be lost. Much of our society is losing its personal connection with the natural world. We are forgetting how to get along with nature. Many of the people who hope to "save" the environment have little first-hand familiarity with it. We don't understand how it works. We don't spend our days trying to fathom how the life, death, and regeneration of humans and other organisms rely on the environment. Most of us don't assume that our households and personal safety are at stake.

Fishing is not a dying industry. It is one that is changing, but it retains hugely important continuities from the past. New England's economy has always relied on an abundance of small, locally owned businesses. We like it that way. It works for us. Changing this would change our entire social structure and culture. People like Maine (or at least find it quaint) because they notice that people here take care of each other, tend to stay put, value their family and cultural heritage, work hard, are clever, and so on. All this is bound up in personal livelihood strategies that rely on local economic networks, in turn based on small, local businesses. This is true of fishing boats and other fishery dependent businesses, as well as other kinds of businesses away from the waterfront. People live here because of what it is, not because of the potential it has for becoming something else. Some people may think this perspective is reactionary, or antiquated, but nothing could be further from the truth. These are conscious choices New Englanders have made after observing the economic paths made by others, and the consequences of those decisions. If we lose our fishing industry, or allow it to consolidate unduly, we lose a big chunk of our soul—as individuals, communities, states, and society at large.

ROGER FLEMING

Attorney

Earthjustice

Appleton, Maine

My views on fisheries are driven by my concern about our future. Although most of us will spend the overwhelming amount of our lives on land surrounded by a world that seems mostly green or maybe brown, we live on a blue planet. Fisheries are one part of a much larger web of life in an ocean world that sustains us, provides us with opportunities for relaxation or adventure, and contributes to our sense of well being, even when we are far from saltwater.

I like to catch fish, eat fish, and I value living in a coastal area where the ocean forms the fabric of everyday life. While I embrace change as part of life, I am simply unable to accept decisions that result in changes to the ocean that will compromise the ability of my son to enjoy the same things that I've been lucky enough to experience. In fact, my hope is that the ocean is in vastly better condition for Miles and his generation when they are my age than it is today. This simple hope is why I do what I do for a living.

The ocean and the fish in the ocean are a public resource. The law, dating back to principles of natural law recorded in ancient times, recognizes that the oceans and the living things they provide belong to all of us. This is true for people whether they live in Iowa or on Isle au Haut. Unfortunately, too often I find this concept gets lost in fisheries management. I respect and am thankful that there are opportunities for commercial and recreational fishermen to catch fish, and I respect the fact that in many circumstances this is how they provide for their families.

I do not always find that the same level of respect is paid to people who value having healthy fish populations in the ocean so there is enough food for other animals like whales or sharks, or so our children's children will have the same chance I've had to catch and eat a codfish or a striped bass. It is also my observation that too often there is a similar lack of respect among fellow fishermen, and I see this lack of respect increasingly directed toward smaller-scale family fishermen.

We need to shift our mindset in fisheries management so that decisions are consistently made with future generations of the public and fishermen in mind. This is reflected in the modern "public trust doctrine," which flows from those simple truths of natural law as old as civilization itself. I hear this concept expressed

often by not just conservationists but from all types of fishermen, fishery managers, scientists, and others involved in fisheries and ocean issues. But too often when decisions are made on the water, around policy-making tables, in our markets, and even in court rooms, not enough of us are honestly living up to this ideal.

I want my son Miles and his children to be able to enjoy everything that a healthy ocean can provide. This includes fish to eat, the joy of seeing a large whale breach the water's surface off the Maine coast, and coastal communities filled with fishermen who share in the responsibility for taking care of our planet's most amazing natural resource.

JERRY SULLIVAN

Owner/Captain

F/V *What's Next?*

Gloucester, Massachusetts

I've been fishing as a hobby since I was a kid. As I got better at fishing, I began selling fish. There were times when work was slow and fishing was good— I depended on fishing for a living. With regulations now, it is becoming difficult to fish from a small boat part-time. There seems to be no clear cut direction fishery management is headed. Right now one of the reasons I fish is to keep my permit, and to afford my twelve-year-old son the opportunity to fish in the future. At times I think the only people that are going to be left fishing are big commercial boats and affluent sports fishermen—with no fish left for the common man!

CLARE GRINDAL

Teacher, Activist

Stonington, Maine

I was brought up on an island over sixty years ago. My father and his friends were fisherman, lobstermen when they could, and would also go seining when they could. People fished whatever was in season then. Now we've lost our way of life and instead it has become a job. In traditional ways you knew what you fished, how you fished, and who you fished with. Everyone has forgotten the ground rules that were set over a hundred years ago. Greed has taken over. We need to bring back the tradition. I do the best that I can to speak for the small fisherman, whether a lobsterman, scalloper, etc. For thirty-five years, I taught these people in schools and I've heard all of their stories of licensing issues, not being able to afford the water-fronts, as well as the other common issues fisherman face. Fisherman are honest, hardworking, "shake hands on it" type of people. Fishing used to be a way of life, meaning that one did whatever it takes, even if it meant getting up at two in the morning to help someone out, not expecting any payment in return. This doesn't happen anymore.

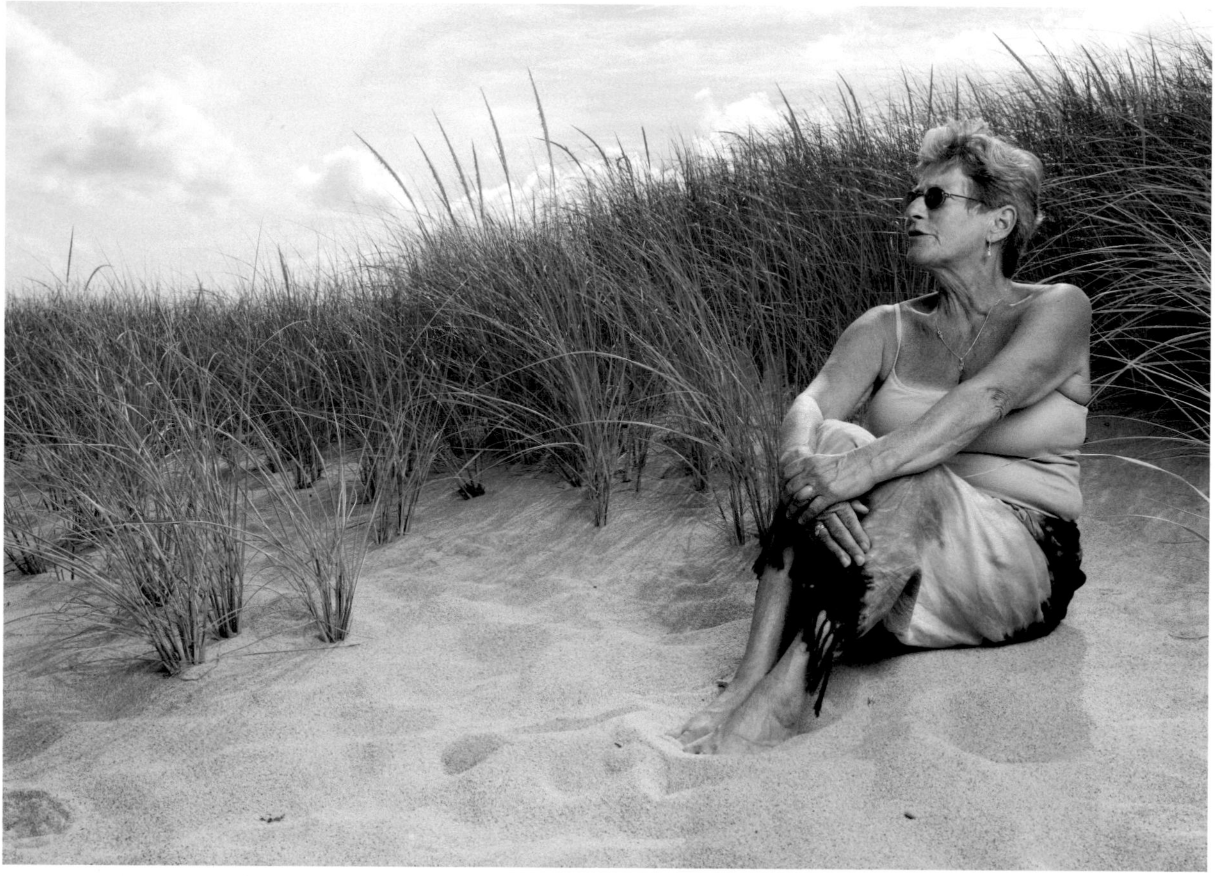

SIMA FRIERMAN

General Manager

Montauk Inlet Seafood

Montauk, New York

I'm a consummate bow rider. I'm sitting here because of my very close ties to individuals who make their livelihoods fishing. Also, I work with the people on the dock and the people in the service industries. The reason I leave my dog at home and get off the dock and sit in this stuffy room is because the passion that I'm hearing in this room is what I hear day in and day out. and these are the people I work for and with. I can take that passion and do something with it. What's really going on is politics. Here we are talking about a fishery that is governed by the NEFMC, where people from Maine have said that over their dead body will New York ever get a seat. I am waiting to see, since southern New England now has a day and a half for every day at sea.... It's politics. When I found out that $16 million in groundfish relief had been granted by the government and that New York doesn't get any, I stomped around the dock—and I am joined by fishermen who are also very angry and pissed off. They have this vessel and their ability to fish has been taken away and they aren't reimbursed for that like the others. I married a fisherman and then I got my MBA in Florida so that I could get a better desk jockey job. I wrote for some publications and did some bookkeeping. Then I got to Montauk. Mid-Atlantic fishermen throw over dead fish because of regulations, unless the squid are on the beach or we're bringing in whiting. I have people come stomping on the dock in June talking about throwing over lots and lots of fish all the time, and that's passion. That's heartbreaking. You've got boats in New York that caught thousands of pounds of fish and now we're looking at wanting a bycatch industry. If four boats go for whiting at the same time, you get 25¢ a pound for it. Herring and mackerel and ilex and butterfish are developing limited access permits. It's truly heartbreaking.

MARK SIMONITSCH

Retired Fisherman and Commercial Pier Owner

Chatham, Massachusetts

Marine resource regulation is and should be fundamentally different from regulating trains, drugs, television, stock exchanges, airlines, and so forth. The marine resource is a finite resource, but has few authentic representatives in the regulatory body that decides its future. Regulation of a finite number of living marine creatures by the very industry that is extracting it from the ocean and dependent on the fish for its income has had deadly consequences for the resource. The regulatory approach we use often permits any activity for which there is no existing regulation. The result is thousands of regulations and still some loopholes remain. People, including the individuals who provide public input, who wish to have any part in making the decisions regarding fish should be held to a very high standard of protection for the resource. No person or group of people should be permitted to engage in any part of the decision-making for the resource if they are not legally committed to the sustainability of the fish.

The idea that the federal government will be the principal protector of the resource is an anachronism. Participants in the legal system of the United States must agree to observing standards and principles of United States' justice. No less should be expected of those who would participate, in any way, to make governance decisions for the marine environment. A better way to protect our marine resource and to also provide for significant economic activity by the industry exploiting the fish would be to govern the industry and fish from the basis of a constitution designed to specifically protect the marine resource. When enfranchised citizens (the fishing industry) are permitted to pursue their own self-interest in government regulatory bodies the outcome is predictable.

More than three hundred years of successful governance experience should influence us to utilize a constitution and to assign and constitutionally guarantee minority rights to the fish resource. Important rights for the unrepresented fish can be given through establishment of institutional internal check and balance mechanisms by a constitution.

The capacity of a governing majority to abuse their power whenever they perceive their selfish interests to be threatened can be constitutionally controlled by procedural devices that are in concert with a resource based set of principals that provide the constitution with its foundation. Procedural considerations along with

institutional structural design can be established by a constitution that will inhibit much of the single-interest advocacy politics that exist and that are un-intensely promoted by the existing regulatory method.

Constitutions are not only well established as the basis for sound governance, but just as importantly they assist government in fulfilling its most important function in those nations where self-government is adopted. The most important function of self governments is to create good citizens who can govern themselves. Resource sustainability is now recognized as an important characteristic of good citizenship. Governance by a specially designed resource-based, constitution will build good citizenship and sustainable resources.

MIKE CROCKER

KAREN CAMPBELL

Director

Women of Fishing Families

Chatham, Massachusetts

I have always been drawn to the ocean. Whether it was spending summers on Ogunquit Beach walking along the Marginal Way or heading to Perkin's Cove to hop aboard the *Finest Kind* for their lobster cruise, the water has continually been where I found peace, solitude, and myself. Looking back, it shouldn't be a surprise that I married a commercial fisherman or that I chose to dedicate my life to protecting the families whose physical and financial well being rely on the ocean's daily gifts. When I began the Women of Fishing Families (W.O.F.F.) non-profit organization, I was determined to support all fishing families, regardless if they made their money from hooks, gillnets, drags, rakes, by hand, or through shoreside support. In speaking to the women of our community, what mattered the most to me was my ability to communicate the one thing we all had in common and translate our unspoken bond into a celebration of the fishing industry. Hours of hard work in adverse conditions, time away from husbands, fathers, brothers, and sons, the feeling in the pit of our stomachs as we watched trucks pull out of driveways in the early hours of the morning and watched boats pull into the dock in the late evening—life in a fishing family is unique and complicated. But it is a lifestyle that I would choose over and over again, and one that I want to honor and respect.

Children of fishing families are nurtured by strong parents and learn about the world through familial and community traditions. After starting my family in a coastal community, I feared that what was once a fishing village saturated with amazing history and tradition had become a town that looked nothing like its former self. Our current profile is not the fault of any one action or individual. As it becomes harder to make a living strictly from the fishing industry, maritime traditions become harder to recall and endure. Many fishermen are forced to seek other sources of income in order to support their families.

W.O.F.F. has the wonderful opportunity to restore these traditions and foster a sense of pride and admiration for a life that is centered around the sea. Women are once again gathering in a common place to provide each other with a rich support system. It is from these women that I draw the courage to promote a fishing industry that keeps us all vibrant and strong willed.

CLIFF GOUDEY

MIT/Sea Grant

Newburyport, Massachusetts

When I was a kid in Maine, my father owned a party boat that he converted from a lobster boat. It was also the family boat and we went out all the time. I don't remember everything, but I've seen pictures of me holding codfish that were bigger than I was. I remember through high school going out to certain places and routinely catch fish. That connection between catching and eating what you caught is so important. I have two young sons and I really want to be able to do that with them some day. I would love to see those kinds of stocks grow back. I don't know how it's going to happen because I don't know if there is a possible way of having stocks that are so generous that they would support that kind of activity and still have a viable commercial fishery. Commercial fishing is the most important thing because recreational fishing is a luxury that I'm not sure we all deserve.

My boys are six and eight, so I can't claim that that's the only reason I care about the future, but they are a renewed reason. I think there's some good that can come from combining some of the skills that I have combined with the skills that fishermen have to find the right solutions. I think that more and more talents have to be brought to the table to develop the right answers.

48; and federal subsidies, 5–6, 19; inshore fleet, 39, 44, 51, 65; management of, 1, 5, 9, 24, 34, 44; offshore fleet, 50, 56, 62, 65; of Pacific Coast, 12; privatization of, 29, 32–34, 66; socio-economic impact of regulations governing, 7, 9–11, 16–17, 39, 44, 52. *See also* groundfish stocks; Magnuson-Stevens Act; management systems; National Marine Fisheries Service.

Fleet Visioning Project, xix, 56–62, 66

Fleming, Roger, 116

flounder, yellowtail, 19–22, 25

Foy, Doug, 39

Freire, Paulo, xx, 55–56

Frierman, Sima, 123

G

Georges Bank, xiv, 19–20, 25, 44

Gilchrest, Wayne, 27

Goethel, David, 73

Goudey, Cliff, 129

Gregg, Judd, 46

Grindal, Clare, 121

groundfish stocks: conservation of, 8, 26, 45; depletion of, v, 6, 15, 23, 28; migrations, 48–49; overfishing, 17, 19–22, 49; recovery of, 5, 10, 17; species management, xviin1, 17, 30; sub–populations of, xiv, xv, 44, 49–50. *See also* specific species.

Gulf of Maine stewardship plan. *See* Inshore Gulf of Maine Fisheries, Conservation and Stewardship Plan.

Gulf of Maine, xiv, 19–20, 25, 45–46, 50

H

haddock, 10, 19–22, 25, 64

hake, 65

Hardin, Garrett, 3–4, 6, 29

Healey, Michael, 6–7

Hennessey, Timothy, 6–7

Hock, Dee, 39–40, 49

Hoskins, Ted, 32

Houghton, Howdy, 107

I

ICNAF. *See* International Commission for Northwest Atlantic Fisheries.

IFISH, 45

IFQ Act of 2001, 32

Inshore Gulf of Maine Fisheries Conservation and Stewardship Plan, The, 49, 53–54

International Commission for Northwest Atlantic Fisheries (ICNAF), 1

Island Institute, 62

K

Kennedy, Ted, 26

Kerry, John, 26, 32, 46

Kessler, Gladys, 51–52

Knauss, John, 5

L

La Valley, Ken, 91

Lauber, Richard, 31

Layzer, Judith, 9

Limited Access Privilege Programs (LAPPS), 34

Longley, James, Jr., 28

Ludwig, Lewis, 6–7

"Ludwig's Ratchet and the Collapse of New England's Groundfish Stocks" (Healey and Hennessey 2000), 6

M

Magnuson, Warren, xxiiin2, 26

Magnuson-Stevens Act: Amendment 4, 17, 39; Amendment 5, 17–19, 46, 53–54; Amendment 9, 51; Amendment 13 (Settlement Agreement), 52–55, 63; Amendment 16, 62, 64; Amendment 17, 64; and biological rebuilding provisions, 52; revision of, xxiiin5, 30, 33–34, 36n57; and 602 guidelines, 17; sixth amendment to, 19; social impacts of, 11

management systems: A-, B- and C-days, 53–54, 63; Apollonio Plan, 24; area-based, xiv, 53, 62–66; Atlantic Demersal Finfish Plan, 24; biological point value, 63–64; community-based, xiii, xxii, 44, 49–50, 55; days-at-sea,

ABOUT NORTHWEST ATLANTIC MARINE ALLIANCE

The Northwest Atlantic Marine Alliance's mission is to restore and enhance an enduring marine system supporting a healthy diversity and an abundance of marine life and human uses through a self-organizing and self-governing organization. For the past decade, we have set the standard for effective collaboration in the pursuit of one question: if we truly care about the health of our oceans does it matter how, where, and when we fish; and, who catches the fish that end up on our dinner plates?

The answer is yes. As eloquently chronicled by Michael Crocker in *Sharing the Ocean*, conventional wisdom and scientific analysis tell us that effective local decision-making processes, local knowledge, and local fishing communities are the key to getting what we need from the ocean in an ecologically responsible and economically sustainable manner.

Based on what we know today, we now set out to answer a new question: How do we facilitate the transition of 1) the market for marine products toward one that is locally based and supports local, small-scale fishermen and fishing communities; and, 2) the decision-making processes toward one that includes community—and ecosystem-based principles?

We thank all of our past and future supporters, collaborators, and funders. In particular, we'd like to thank the Andrus Family Fund for making *Sharing the Oceans* possible.

—Niaz Dorry, Coordinating Director
Northwest Atlantic Marine Alliance
April 2008

To ensure this book doesn't add to the burden of our oceans, communities, and environment, and to support local businesses, we chose to work with two Maine-based businesses: Tilbury House, Publishers and J. S. McCarthy, Printers. We are thankful to both for their work and support. We chose our printer because of their exceptional commitment to a better world which includes: using 100 percent wind power at their facilities; an aggressive recycling policy; employing non-hazardous vegetable-based inks; using wood pulp from forests certified by the Forest Stewardship Council; and, adopting an effective toxic-use-reduction strategy. These decisions have a direct impact on the marine ecosystem. In addition, this book is printed on elemental chlorine-free paper, thus reducing the amount of persistent and bio-accumulative chlorine-based toxins, especially dioxins. When such compounds enter our environment, they are known to adversely impact reproductive capabilities and overall health of marine animals and humans.